Jiang Rongqiao's Baguazhang

姜容樵的
八卦掌

Available from tgl books
Jiang Rongqiao's Baguazhang
Li Tianji's The Skill of Xingyiquan
Yan Dehua's Bagua Applications
Di Guoyong on Xingyiquan: Volume I, Foundations
Di Guoyong on Xingyiquan: Volume II, Forms and Ideas
Di Guoyong on Xingyiquan: Volume III, Weapons
A Shadow on Fallen Blossoms
Falk's Dictionary of Chinese Martial Arts
Beijing Bittersweet
Shadowboxing in Shanghai

tgl books   www.thewushucentre.ca

Jiang Rongqiao's Baguazhang

Chinese-English Edition

姜容樵的八卦掌
汉英对照版

A translation from the Chinese
by Andrea Mary Falk

霍安娣翻译，主板

First Printing of Chinese-English Edition: 2019.
Published by tgl books, Québec, Canada.

Library and Archives Canada Cataloguing in Publication of first translation edition
Chiang, Jung-ch'iao. Jiang Rongqiao's Baguazhang. Translation of: Baguazhang. 1.
Hand-to-hand fighting, Oriental. I. Title. II. Baguazhang.
GV1112.C5513   2000 796.815'5   C00-910847-5

This translation is of "Baguazhang" by Jiang Rongqiao.
Published originally in 1963, reprinted 1980,
People's Sport Publishing House, Beijing, China.
First translated by Andrea Falk, 1989, Vancouver, Canada.
Photographs posed by Cai Yuhua and taken by Andrea Falk, 1990, Shanghai.
First printed 1992 as cerloxed booklet. The first published edition was 2000. Second
edition, 2003. The third Edition is the Chinese-English Edition, 2019.
The techniques described in this book are intended for experienced martial artists.
The author, translator, and publishers are not responsible for any injury that may
occur while trying out these techniques. Please do not apply these techniques on
anyone without their consent and cooperation.

tgl books is based in Canada. Its publications are available through
www.thewushucentre.ca.

Thanks to my sifu, Huan Dahai (1924-2015), for teaching me Jiang Rongqiao's baguazhang.

Contents

Translator's Preface

This book has always been one of my favourites because of professor Jiang Rongqiao's clear explanation of training methods and the dynamic drawings of his postures. I learned his style from my sifu Huan Dahai, one of his students in Shanghai, and from my martial elder brother, Cai Yuhua. I believe that the photos that I took of Cai Yuhua give the feel of the style's energy even more than the drawings. Some of the photos differ from the drawings because we did not copy the book exactly, but went by what Cai Yuhua had learned from our sifu.

Some terminology that may be confusing to the reader unused to sports terminology:

1) Medial rotation: if the arm were hanging beside the body with the palm facing the leg, medial rotation would turn the forearm so that the palm faced to the back. When in different positions, it is helpful to think of turning the thumb in towards the palm.

2) Lateral rotation: if the arm were hanging beside the body with the palm facing the leg, lateral rotation would turn the forearm so that the palm faced the front. When in different positions, it is helpful to think of turning the little finger in towards the palm.

Thanks to Xia Bohua, in Beijing, and Huan Dahai and Cai Yuhua, in Shanghai, for teaching me Jiang Rongqiao's baguazhang. Thanks again to Cai Yuhua for the long hot day posing. Thanks also to Liang Shouyu, in Vancouver, for explaining the more exotic movement names.

Any mistakes in the book are mine alone. I hope that you like this book as much as I, and apologize for the fact a translation is never as good as the original.

Andrea Mary Falk 霍安娣

Victoria, Canada, 2000

Preface to the Chinese-English Edition

I typed out this Chinese-English edition in 2015 to celebrate the 50th anniversary of the original Chinese edition of this book. The setup up is simple – first the Chinese, then the English. I waited until the stock of the the previous edition sold out before making this edition available, but now here it is. Typing in Chinese is fraught with possibilities of incorrect entry, so please excuse any mistaken characters that I missed in proof reading.

Since I did the first translation I have been lucky in studying the old eight changes with other Jiang style teachers, a little bit with Jiang Rongqiao's adoptive daughter Zou Shuxian, one long session with Sha Guozheng's special disciple Su Zifang, a short session with her son Zhao Yun, and mostly with my martial eldest brother Cheng Jiefeng. The differences and similarities to my original learning with my sifu Huan Dahai and martial elder brother Cai Yuhua reinforced my understanding of Jiang style. This gave me the confidence to add a few notes to the original translation. In passing, I of course changed the translation slightly. I just can't help it. I renumbered the images and photos, and shifted things around a bit to make more sense to the way we train the changes. I also deleted the pointers on the repeated side, as they just repeated what was already said on the first side.

The more I look into Jiang Rongqiao's life and literary output the more I respect him as a martial artist and person, and the prouder I am to be in his lineage. In addition to his bagua, I also train a Taiji Changquan that he transmitted to my sifu and to Cheng Jiefeng. I hope to publish a book on this if I get permission.

The drawings of this book were done from photos taken when Jiang was older, so the power flow is clearly visible but the stances aren't as flashy as in his younger years. I have put in some photos from the 1930s in the introduction, to show the flavour of his unique skill.

There is something about these old eight changes, I never get tired of them. I also love working with the drawings of Jiang Rongqiao and photos of Cai Yuhua. Their skill is evident in every single pose, and they are a joy to look at. Although this is a short and relatively simple book, I think it is useful to people who love baguazhang, and well worth bringing out again, with the addition of the original Chinese.

Andrea Mary Falk 霍安娣

Québec, Canada

May, 2019

Preface to the 20th Anniversary hard cover editions

At this 20th anniversary of the establishment of tgl books, I have finally completed the reworking of all the books to be available for print to order. To celebrate, I have made hard cover copies of all the translations – the Li Tianji, Yan Dehua, and Di Guoyong books, as well as this one. In setting up the hard cover editions, I of course made a few minor changes, but the translations are all in their final state now. If there are any remaining mistakes, that is just too bad.

Andrea Mary Falk 霍安娣

Québec, Canada

February, 2021

About the Author

Professor Jiang Rongqiao 姜容樵 (1891-1974, alternate name Guangwu 光武) was born into a martial arts family in Hebei province, in the North of China. His father, Jiang Tingju 姜廷举, was a master teacher of Mizong boxing 秘宗拳, so young Jiang started training Mizong very early. His formal education was not neglected, though – he was given a classical education with a tutor at home. He was talented in his training, and was said to be especially proficient in hard whip and sword. In 1909 he apprenticed with master Zhang Zhangui 张占魁 to learn Bagua and Xingyi. He also learned Taishi whip 太师鞭 from Li Yusan 李雨三, Taijiquan from his good friend Tang Shilin 汤士林, and Wudang sword 武当剑 from Li Jinglin 李景林. He

trained seriously and always wanted to understand the theory and application of techniques. As Li Jinglin described him, "He has a lively attitude and perfectly combines hard and soft – he has no dead spots or purely hard spots. He is a real asset to the martial scene. And to top it off, he is good at theoretical studies."

In the 1920's, while Jiang worked for the Tianjin-Shanghai railway, he started to teach martial arts. In 1928 he formed the Association to Achieve

Virtue by Esteeming the Martial 尚武进德会 in Shanghai and started to write books to spread the martial arts. In 1932 he was made director of the editorial department of the National Martial Arts Centre 中央国术馆 in Nanjing, where he was responsible for writing and editing, but also had time for teaching. He left when the Japanese attacked, and spent years as a teacher of literature and history, but never stopped teaching martial arts. He later moved back to Shanghai where he lived out his retirement. In

his later years he concentrated on
research and writing, and continued to
teach even as his eyesight failed.

What made Jiang Rongjiao exceptional
was that his excellence in performance
was matched by his desire and ability to
teach and write. He dedicated his whole
life to spreading the martial arts and reached many people through direct
teaching and his many books. Among his books are: *A Description of
Qingping Sword* 写真青萍剑, *A Description of the Mother Fists of Xingyi* 写真
形意母拳, *Xingyi Mixture of Moves and Eight Postures* 形意杂式捶八式拳合刊, *A
Description of Mizong Boxing* 写真秘宗拳, *Depiction of Bagua Invisible Spear*
八卦奇门枪, *Teaching Materials for Taijiquan* 太极拳术讲义, *A Description of
Taishi Tiger Tail Whip* 写真太师虎尾鞭, *Taishi Waterstone Whip* 太师水磨鞭, *A
Description of Fighting with Whip and Spear* 写真鞭枪大战, *Kunwu Sword* 昆
吾剑, *Shaolin Staff Techniques* 少林棍法, and *Tales of Present Day Martial
Heroes* 当代武人奇侠传.

(Information collected from a variety of wushu encyclopedias. Photos from
books written by Jiang Rongqiao in the 1930s.)

Author's Preface

八卦掌，是以掌法和步法的变换转行为中心的拳术套路。它的基本掌法是：单换掌，双换掌，双撞掌，穿掌，挑掌，翻身掌，摇身掌，转身掌等八掌。它的基本步法是：起，落，扣，摆等四种。

Baguazhang is a style of wushu that holds at its core ever changing circular palm techniques and footwork. Its basic palm techniques include: single change palm [dān huàn zhǎng], double change palm [shuāng huàn zhǎng], double ramming palm [shuāng zhuàng zhǎng], piercing palm [chuān zhǎng], rising palm [tiǎo zhǎng], body rolling palm [fān shēn zhǎng], body shaking palm [yáo shēn zhǎng], and body spinning palm [zhuàn shēn zhǎng], among others. Its basic footwork includes: lift [qǐ], land [luò], hook in [kòu], and turn out [bǎi], among others.

八卦掌可以就其八掌中的一掌单独练习，也可以把八掌贯串起来先后穿插地连环练习。

Baguazhang can be practiced by working on each change individually or by flowing the eight changes together.

八卦掌的运动特点是：一走，二视，三坐，四翻。这些特点为发展身手的轻捷，灵活，特别是下肢的力量提供了必要的锻炼条件。通过八卦掌的锻炼，将会给我们带来健康。

The characteristics of baguazhang movement are: walk [zǒu], look [shì], sit [zuò], and roll [fān]. These characteristics develop the agility and quickness of the body and hands, and especially create conditions to greatly train the strength of the legs. Training baguazhang greatly benefits our health.

八卦掌最早的来源，不知起于何时。在《蓝籍外史》"靖边记"里却有这样的记载："嘉庆丁已（嘉庆二年），有山东济宁人王祥教冯克善拳法，克善尽得其术。庚午春（嘉庆十五年），牛亮臣见克善拳法中有八方步，亮臣曰尔步似合八卦。克善曰：子何以知之？亮臣曰：我所习坎卦。克善曰：我为离卦。尔为离，我为坎，我二人离坎交宫，各习其所习可也。"从这里可以看出八卦掌传溜到今天，至少也有一百多年了。

The earliest roots of baguazhang are unknown. There are references in the Record of Pacifying the Borders of The History of the Blue Register (a historical romance based loosely on fact) that state "In 1797, Wangxiang, from Jining in Shandong, taught martial arts to Feng Keshan. In 1811, Niu Liangchen saw Keshan's martial art and noticed that that its footwork had eight directions. He remarked that the footwork resembled the eight trigrams. Keshan asked how he recognized that. Liangchen replied that he studied the *kan* trigram. Kechan said that he did the *li* trigram. Liangchen then said that since one did *li* and the other did *kan*, the two of them should learn from each other and combine the two opposite trigrams." From this it can be seen that baguazhang has a history of at least a hundred years.

清道光中叶以后至光绪六年，是八卦掌发展最盛的时期。北京一带，学习八卦掌的人颇多。八卦掌前辈董海川先生是当时传授八卦掌的主要人物，从其学者有程廷华，尹福，宋长荣，张占魁等。

Baguazhang flourished in the period around 1820 to 1880, and was especially popular in the Beijing area. The person largely responsible for teaching baguazhang during that time was Dong Haichuan. Well known students of his include Cheng Tinghua, Yin Fu, Song Changrong and Zhang Zhankui, among others.

我从张占魁先生学习有年，粗知梗概，当此体育运动空前发展之际，颇愿将自己所学之八卦掌贡献给大家，作为炼身体的方法。为此编写成书，然而由于对八卦掌尚缺乏深刻的研究，不免会存在许多缺点，尚望读者多提宝贵意见，以便今后改正。

I studied with master Zhang Zhankui (Zhang Zhaodong) for years and have some rough understanding of this skill. In this sport conscious time, I feel it is my duty to write of the baguazhang that I have learned, to present to everyone for them to use to develop their bodies. For this reason I have written this book. I have not researched baguazhang in depth, so there are many shortcomings. I hope it is of use, even with its shortcomings. I invite readers to send their valuable suggestions in order to correct and improve the book in the future.

姜容樵
Jiang Rongqiao

Part One
八 卦 掌 的 锻 炼 方 法
The Training Methods of Baguazhang

顺 项 提 顶、 溜 臀 收 肛;

shùn xiàng tí dǐng, liú tún shōu gāng;

Straighten the neck and lift the head, tuck in the buttocks and close the anal sphincter;

松 肩 沉 肘、 实 腹 畅 胸;

sōng jiān chén zhǒu, shí fù chàng xiōng;

Relax the shoulders and sink the elbows, solidify the abdomen and let the chest remain unobstructed;

滚 钻 争 裹、 奇 正 相 生;

gǔn zuān zhēng guǒ, qí zhèng xiāng shēng;

Roll and screw, contend and wrap, create opposing forces;

龙 形 猴 相、 虎 坐 鹰 翻;

lóng xíng hóu xiàng, hǔ zuò yīng fān;

Have a dragon shape and a monkey manner, crouch like a tiger and roll like an eagle;

拧 旋 走 转、 蹬 脚 摩 胫;

níng xuán zǒu zhuàn, dēng jiǎo mó jìng;

Twist and rotate, walk and turn, drive the foot and scrape the shin;

曲 腿 蹚 泥、 足 心 涵 空;

qū tuǐ tāng ní, zú xīn hán kōng;

Bend the legs and walk as if wading through mud, keep the centre of the feet hollow;

起 平 落 扣、 连 环 纵 横;

qǐ píng luò kòu, lián huán zòng héng;

Lift flat and land tucked in, connect to the length and breadth;

腰 如 轴 立、 手 似 轮 行;

yāo rú zhóu lì, shǒu sì lún xíng;

The waist is like an erect axle, the hands turn like wheels;

1

指　分　掌　凹、　摆　肱　平　肩；
zhǐ　fēn　zhǎng　aō,　bǎi　gōng　píng　jiān;

The fingers are open and the palms concave, the arms swing with the shoulders level;

桩　如　山　岳、　步　似　水　中；
zhuāng　rú　shān　yuè,　bù　sì　shuǐ　zhōng;

Stand like a mountain, walk like flowing water;

火　上　水　下、　水　重　火　轻；
huǒ　shàng　shuǐ　xià,　shuǐ　zhòng　huǒ　qīng;

Be like fire above and water below, water is heavy and fire is light;

意　如　瓢　旗、　又　如　点　灯；
yī　rú　piāo　qí,　yòu　sì　diǎn　dēng;

Intention is like an army pennant or signal lantern;

腹　乃　气　根、　气　似　云　行；
fù　nǎi　qì　gēn,　qì　sì　yún　xíng;

The abdomen is the root of the energy, the breath moves like clouds;

意　动　生　慧、　气　行　百　孔；
yì　dòng　shēng　huì,　qì　xíng　bǎi　kǒng;

When the mind is active it creates intelligence and energy moves to the hundred cavities;

展　放　收　紧、　动　静　圆　撑；
zhǎn　fàng　shōu　jǐn,　dòng　jìng　yuán　chēng;

Open out expansively and gather in tightly, movement and stillness are part of a continuous circle;

神　气　意　力、　合　一　集　中；
shén　qì　yì　lì,　hé　yī　jí　zhōng;

Combine and concentrate the spirit, energy, intention and strength;

八　掌　真　理、　俱　在　此　中。
bā　zhǎng　zhēn　lǐ,　jù　zài　cǐ　zhōng.

The truth of baguazhang is found in the above.

顺项提顶，溜臀收肛。顺项是使颈项自然竖直，在锻炼时不要仰头，不要低头，也不要左右歪斜；提顶是将下颔里收，头向上直顶；溜臀是将臀部下垂向里收缩，在锻炼时不要有丝毫的向后撅臀的现象产生；收肛是将肛门的肌肉予以收缩控制，不要使它放松。

Straighten the neck and lift the head, tuck in the buttocks and close the anal sphincter. Straightening the neck means to hold the neck naturally erect. When training, the head must not tilt back, drop forward, or tilt to either side. Lift the head means to pull in the chin slightly so that the crown of the head is lifted up. Tuck in the buttock means to keep the pelvis tucked in. When training, the buttock does not stick out the slightest amount. Close the anal sphincter means to contract the muscles in the anal sphincter, so that it is not lax.

Translator's note: Holding in the buttocks and anal sphincter means to keep your central area firm – it does not mean to hold yourself rigid or in a strong pelvic tilt. Once this straight position becomes normal, you can expand from the lower back and ribcage area to get more power and ensure that you won't hurt your back during a throw. The sphincter is closed with the same energy you would use to close your eyes.

松肩沉肘，实腹畅胸。松肩是使两肩向下松沉，在锻炼时不要向上耸肩；沉肘是使肘部经常保持向下沉坠，在锻炼时必须屈如半月形；腹是"蓄气"的良好部位，实腹就是指在锻炼时必须将呼吸深入到腹部，使腹部充实鼓荡，既所谓"气沉丹田"，"内宜鼓荡"的意思；胸部的向外挺凸，固然会影响"气沉丹田"，而胸部的向里收缩，也足以影响到心脏的压缩，阻碍了血液流畅，因之，畅胸就是指胸部要宽松开展，既不要挺胸也不要缩胸。

Relax the shoulders and sink the elbows, solidify the abdomen and let the chest remain unobstructed. Relax the shoulders means to settle the shoulders down. When training, never shrug them. Sink the elbows means to keep the elbows in a position pointing down. When training, keep them bent in a crescent shape. The abdomen is an excellent place to store *qi*, or energy, so solidifying the abdomen means to pull the breath down into the lower abdomen, which makes it solid, which is also called settling the energy into the *dantian*, or 'swelling the internal drum'. If the chest is puffed out this will naturally affect the ability to sink the energy to the dantian, and if the chest is collapsed, this will affect the contraction of the heart, and thus impede blood flow. So an unobstructed chest means to keep the chest open and relaxed, neither puffed out nor collapsed in.

Translator's note: All of these postural habits ensure that your centre of gravity stays low, so you will be more effective in throwing techniques. In addition, keeping the shoulders, elbows and chest set down and relaxed allows the lower back to connect directly to the arms through the natural lines of the muscles, tendons and ligaments.

滚钻争裹，奇正相生。这是指锻炼时的劲力变化而言。滚是圆形的旋臂动作，钻是既要转又要相前的螺旋形的旋臂动作，争是向外撑开，裹是向里扣抱。这四种动作在运动时都必须使肌肉收缩产生力量。仅仅是圆形的滚转，没有向前的力量，这种劲力的里面没有向外和向前的劲力矛盾，力量不能保持最大，因之在锻炼的时候，必须要滚中带钻，使圆形的滚钻动作成为螺旋形的动作。争和裹也是这个意思，两臂肘的合抱固然该使用裹力，但是裹力只有向里收的劲，而没有向外扩张的劲，这里面就没有向里和向外的劲力矛盾产生，如果是裹里带争，这里面就有了收缩和扩张的对抗性，就有了劲力的矛盾产生。奇正两字，是代表着二种不同性质的事务的矛盾。"奇正相生"换句话说，也就是"矛盾产生了"。八卦掌的一切劲力，都是由滚，钻，争，裹四力的相互对抗，在奇正的矛盾产生中所发挥出来的。

Roll and screw, contend and wrap, create opposing forces. This refers to the changes in the application of power during performance. Roll is a rounded rotational movement of the arms. Screw is a spiraling rotational movement of the arms, which turns while moving forward. Contend is to press out. Wrap is to hold something in. These four actions must all create strength by muscular contractions. If a rounded rolling motion does not contain forward strength, this kind of power does not contain the contradictory outward and forward power, so the strength cannot be maintained at its peak. When performing the roll, it must contain a screwing or drilling action, so the rounded rolling action contains a spiraling action. Contending and wrapping also have the same implication. Although the arms and elbows hold in and stabilize during the wrap, if the wrap power does not contain an opening out power there will be no inward and outward opposition in forces. Contending should be contained in wrapping, so there will be both contraction and expansion, creating an oppositional power. It is desirable to create oppositional powers. All of the power in baguazhang comes from the opposition of the four types of power – roll, screw, contend and wrap.

Translator's note: Always pressuring in opposing directions puts the opponent in a difficult position when you have a hold on him – you can pull him off balance while maintaining good balance yourself. Keeping a pressure away from yourself even when pulling in prevents your opponent from being pulled into you or from trying to drive into you.

龙形猴相，虎坐鹰翻。这是指锻炼时的身形，身法，步法的变化而言。八卦掌的运动特点之一就是"走"，这种滔滔不绝的圆形步，必须使之"形如游龙"，悠然之中含着稳重；八卦掌的运动特点之二是"视"，八卦掌在转行时或转身换掌时，两眼总是注视着两掌，所谓"手眼相随"，眼是心的苗，"视"能显示出运动的内在精神，这种精神必须使之象猿猴守物那样灵之中含着警惕意味，并通过眼的注视把它表达出来；八卦掌的运动特点之三是"坐"，在转行时，它的两腿并不伸直，采用"坐跨"，在转身换掌时的一顿之间又有"坐桩"的动作，这些蹲坐的动作和腿法，必须使之象"虎踞"之形，沉着有力；八卦掌的运动特点之四是"翻"，就是转身的动作，在转身时必须采取鹞鹰盘旋空中翻身降落的那种灵敏，洒脱之势。

Have a dragon shape and monkey manner, crouch like a tiger and roll like an eagle. This explains the body shape, body technique and footwork. The first characteristic of baguazhang is walking. This continuous circular walking must be done like a swimming dragon, that is, it must be stable and solid while moving quickly. The second characteristic of baguazhang is looking. While walking or turning, the eyes keep on the hands, so that it seems like the eyes and hands are following each other. The eyes are the windows to the spirit, and looking shows the spirit within the movements. This spirit shown in the eyes should be lively and attentive like a monkey hunting. The third characteristic of baguazhang is sitting. While moving, the legs never fully straighten, and the hip joints are always sitting. Within the turning and changing is stake sitting, this squatting is combined with leg techniques, so should be like a tiger, settled and strong. The fourth characteristic of baguazhang is rolling. That is, while the body is turning, it should be as agile and sudden as an eagle soaring in the sky then suddenly rolling over and dropping to earth.

Translator's note: When dragons appear in Chinese literature they arrive with a big rush of wind and noise. Being caught by a dragon-like baguazhang player would be like being suddenly caught up in a washing machine, you wouldn't know what had hold of you. Sitting like a tiger is similarly a very apt metaphor. Any cat can sit for hours waiting for a prey to appear, and still be able to strike instantaneously. This suggests that when practicing, especially when practicing standing, you must always be just on the verge of moving although it doesn't look like that from the outside. Standing practice in this way keeps the muscles from getting tense and 'muscle-bound' and keeps the mind alert.

拧旋走转，蹬脚摩胫。拧旋走转就是说在走转时必须是腰要拧，肘臂要拧，手掌要拧，颈项要拧，使头手肘身拧向圆心的一面，拧成一股旋劲；蹬脚摩胫，是指在走转时前行之脚必须轻迈，后行之脚必须蹬劲；向前进步必须贴近前脚胫骨里侧摩擦而过，不要将脚提得过高或过宽。

Twist and rotate, walk and turn, drive the foot and scrape the shin. Twist and rotate means that while walking the waist should twist, the elbows and arms should twist, the hands and palms should twist, and the neck should twist, so that the head, hands, elbows and body twist to face the center of the circle. This twisting creates a rotational power. Drive the foot means that when walking, the front foot must stride lightly while the back foot pushes forward forcibly. When advancing, the moving foot must pass close by the supporting leg, scraping the shin, lifting neither too high nor too wide.

Translator's note: The specific word used to say drive the foot forward reminds you to drive with the whole foot, pushing from behind the ball of the foot. The emphasis on controlling the placement of the shins keeps the whole leg under control from the hips. Stop the moving foot by the supporting foot, touching the instep on the anklebone. This will keep your whole step solid. If you concentrate on just keeping your knees together you can still lose your balance easily.

曲腿蹚泥，足心涵空。曲腿就是在走转时两腿作适度之弯曲，身体往下坐，使力量贯注两腿；蹚泥是两脚前进不要过高，如蹚泥之壮；足心涵空是使两脚掌和脚跟同时平落地面，五趾抓地，这样脚心就涵空了。

Bend the legs and walk as if wading through mud, keep the centre of the feet hollow. Bend the legs means that while walking the legs keep flexed so that the body remains crouching or sitting, which keeps the strength in the legs. Wade through mud means to keep the feet close to the ground when they move forward. The soles of the feet are hollow means that the whole of the foot lands at the same time, with the toes gripping the ground, which makes the sole the foot hollow.

Translator's note: Don't curl your toes, as this puts you off balance, but grab from the ball of the foot, so that the meat of the toes grips the ground.

起平落扣，连环纵横。起平是将脚提起时也要象"足心涵空"那样平；落扣是说落步时不仅要平落，还要使脚里扣；连环是不断的意思，意识不断，劲力不断，动作不断，从连环中生出纵横，上下左右四面八方一气连环。

Lift flat and land tucked in, connect to the length and breadth. Lift flat means to keep the flat, hollow shape of the foot when lifting it. Land tucked in means that in landing, not only does the foot land flat, but also hooks in. Connected means that there is no break – intent does not break, power does not break, and movement does not break – they are continuous. From this connectedness all directions are covered – lengthways and sideways, up and down, left and right, the four sides and eight directions.

Translator's note: The landing can also be translated as concave, that is, with the foot gripping the ground. Placing the foot with this control ensures that the whole body will be balanced and connected.

腰如轴立，手似轮行。八卦掌在锻炼时必须以腰部构成运动的轴心，手动必先身动，身动必先腰动，使腰带动一切；八卦掌在换掌的时候必须使手臂的动作如车轮那样形成圆圈，因为圆形动转较为灵敏，又含着连环不断的作用。

The waist is like an erect axle, the hands turn like wheels. When training, the waist must form the axis of movement, so that to move the hands the body moves first, and to move the body the waist moves first. The waist leads all movement. When performing the changes the arm movements follow the waist like the circular movements of a wheel, because this type of movement is agile and continuous.

Translator's note: The waist means the whole lower back, kidney area, inside the body, not just the external muscles, waist where you measure the waist, or spine.

指分掌凹，摆肱平肩。指分是将五指分开，不要并拢，掌凹是使掌心向里涵空凹拢；摆肱是在转行时两臂必须极力向圆心的一面摆动，不可有向前推的动作；平肩是两肩在转行时或转身时都必须保持正平舒，不要一起一落的现象。

The fingers are open and the palms concave, the arms swing with the shoulders level. Open the fingers means that the fingers and thumb are spread rather than held together. A concave palm means that there is a concavity or hollowed place in the centre of the palm. Swing the arms means that when walking the circle the arms must swing to the centre of the circle rather than pushing out to the front. The shoulders level means that the shoulders always stay level and settled down when moving the arms or turning the body. They must never lift or drop.

Translator's note: Opening the fingers and keeping pressure in the palms keeps the muscles of the arms solid so that they are not crushed if an arm technique is used. It also sends energy to the tips of the arm, which keeps the whole arm alive.

桩如山岳，步似水中。桩是指静止性的动作，八卦掌的桩步必须使之象山岳那样稳固，似乎任何强大的力量都推它不动似的；步是指活动性的动作，八卦掌的"趟泥步"必须使之在稳健之中含着象流水那样轻快，这样八卦掌的步法就不是笨重的，也不是浮漂的了。

Stand like a mountain, walk like flowing water. When stopped, the body must be absolutely stable, like a mountain, as if nothing could budge it. Walking with the mud wading step must be as light and fast as flowing water while remaining steady. In this way the footwork will be neither heavy nor floating.

火上水下，水重火轻。心在上属火，肾在下属水，所谓"心火肾水"，也就是前面所说"实腹畅胸"的心要虚，腹要实的意思。

Be like fire above and water below, water is heavy and fire is light. The heart, which is above, is classified as fire, and the kidneys, which are below, are classified as water, so this phrase means the same as keeping the abdomen solid and the chest unobstructed. That is, the chest area is empty and the abdomen is solid.

意如飘旗，又似点灯。古代练兵，一切的阵形变化，前进后退都必须以飘荡的令旗和夜间灯为引导，八卦掌运动时也必须以意识引导动作，不能随随便便地运动。

Intention is like an army pennant or signal lantern. In ancient times, all army maneuvers followed a pennant by day and a lantern by night for directions. This phrase means that the movement of baguazhang must follow the orders of the mind, movement is made with full intent, not randomly.

Translator's note: The phrase also suggests that each movement must have a purpose, as army orders are given to follow definite plans of attack or defense. If you don't know the practical purpose you won't have the correct application of power in the movements.

腹乃气根，气似云行。前面已经说过腹是"蓄气"的良好部位，在锻炼时必须将呼吸之气深入到腹部，但是这种深呼吸的运动是猛然一口就将气吸入腹内呢，还是慢慢地吸入呢？"气似云行"就说明了八卦掌的深呼吸运动必须是象空中行云那样慢慢地运行，不要猛然吸入，也不要猛然呼出。

The abdomen is the root of the energy, the breath moves like clouds. It has already been explained that since the abdomen is an excellent place to store energy or air, the breath must be pulled down to the abdomen. But does this type of deep breathing mean to suddenly suck a large breath down to the belly or to slowly inhale? The breath moves like clouds means that the deep breath must be like the clouds moving slowly through the sky – do not abruptly inhale, and do not abruptly exhale.

意动生慧，气行百孔。意动生慧是说八卦掌的运动如果是象前面说说的"意如飘旗，又如点灯"那样有意识的运动，那么就能在运动中培养出机警，敏感的素质。气行百孔是说如果八卦掌的深呼吸是按照前面所说的"气似云行"那样的话，那么所吸入的氧气就能输送到各个需要的地方去。

When the mind is active it creates intelligence and the energy moves to the hundred cavities. If the mind acts as the aforementioned 'guiding pennant or lantern' when training, then training baguazhang will develop the qualities of intelligence and sensitivity. Also, since deep breathing moves the aforementioned 'qi moves like clouds', then training baguazhang will bring oxygen to every part of the body where it is needed.

展放收紧，动静圆撑。展放收紧是指动作姿势的开合而言，开的姿势要舒展远放，合的姿势要内收外紧；动静圆撑是指动中必须求静，静中又必须有动；动的极处就是静的发源，静的极处就是动的起端，这动和静必须相互循行，又相互含蓄。

Open out expansively and close in tightly, movement and stillness are part of a continuous circle. Open movements must be expansive with full amplitude, and closed movements must be tight and closed in. Stillness is contained in moving and movement is implicit in stillness. The endpoint of action is the origin of inaction and the endpoint of inaction is the origin of action. Thus movement and stillness draw on each other and contain each other.

Translator's note: The continuation is due to the elasticity of the body. The sequence of the movements in Jiang's baguazhang form is linked so well together that if each move is done to its full extent, it will spring naturally to the following move.

神气意力，合一集中。前面所说到的精神，气息，意识，力量等等各方面的锻炼方法，它们并不是独立的，而是合一集中的，不集中，动作就不能完整一气，不合一手脚就不能行动一致。所谓"合一"，就是手与脚合，肩与胯合，肘与膝合，神与意合，气与力合，内与外合；所谓"集中"，就是这六合必须统一，和谐，协调，取得完整。

Combine and concentrate the spirit, energy, intention and strength. The above explanations of how to train the spirit, energy, intention and strength are not independent of each other, but are combined. If they are not combined, then movements cannot be completed in one breath. If the hands and feet do not combine, then action is unconcerted. Combining all of them leads to developing technique that moves as one unit – the hands and feet are as one, the shoulders and hips are as one, the elbows and knee are as one, the spirit and intention are as one, the energy and strength are as one, and the internal and external are as one. Concentrated means that only when these six harmonies occur is the body coordinated and complete.

八掌真理，俱在此中。这是说如果完全掌握和运用了上面所说的八卦掌的锻炼方法，才算得到了八卦掌的真正的技术，不然的话，那还是只算学会了一套空架子而已。

The truth of baguazhang is found in the above. Only by mastering and using these principles can skill in baguazhang be achieved. If not, one is only moving around in an empty form.

八卦掌的三个锻炼步骤
The Three Stages of Training of Baguazhang

八卦掌的锻炼，分为三个步骤，就是：定架子，活架子，变架子。第一步骤，一定要先练定架子，这是八卦掌打基础的步骤。定架子就是一步一趋，慢慢地，规规矩矩地按八卦掌的动作练习。不可快。

Baguazhang training can be separated into three stages. That is: set frames [dìng jiàzǐ], moving frames [huó jiàzǐ], and changing frames [biàn jiàzǐ]. In the first stage, set frames must be trained, to prepare the foundation. To practice set frames means to perform each step and each move slowly and carefully, performing it exactly according to the requirements. Practice in this stage cannot be rushed.

第二步骤，是活架子。活架子是步法不停的练习。换式时，不要把步法停住，应迅速向前迈出去，每式都如此换步，就完全变成活的步法了。八卦掌的活架子，走起来如游龙，如飞凤，妖妖娇娇，非常美观好看。

The second stage is moving frames. To practice moving frames means to practice without stopping. When performing the changes, the footwork never stops, and movements flow quickly from one to the other. Every posture moves from one to the other with moving footwork. The moving frame practice of baguazhang looks like a swimming dragon or a flying phoenix, gentle and lovely – very beautiful to watch.

第三步骤是变架子。变架子是随意变化，有时把第一掌放在最后练，有时把第八掌作第一掌练，有时把第四掌作第二掌练，这样随意穿插练习，就可以千变万化，无穷无尽，越练越多。

The third stage is changing frames. This means to perform the changes in random order as you please, mixing up the order, sometimes doing the first change last, the eighth change first, the fourth change second, or whatever you want. In this way training is never the same twice and the changes are endless.

八卦掌的三盘
The Three Basins of Baguazhang

八卦掌分上盘，中盘，和下盘三种练法，通称三盘练法。上盘练法是：身体直立，走起步法来，就象寻常人走路一样，不向下坐胯。中盘练法是：两腿屈膝微蹲，上半身与腰部的重点落于两腿上，走起步法来，就象蹚泥蹚水一般。上盘和中盘练法以走快步最相宜。下盘练法是八卦掌的最困难的练法，它必须是：腿极力弯曲，脚跟与臀部，膝盖要成一个三角形。全身的重点落在两腿上，走步越慢越好。

Baguazhang can be done in upper basin, middle basin, or lower basin training methods. In practicing the high basin the body is straight and upright and the walking is almost like normal walking, that is, not sitting down into the hip joints. In the middle basin the legs are bent and the center of gravity of the torso and lumbar region settle over the legs. The walking is just like wading in mud or water. The high and middle basin methods are most appropriate for a fast walk. The low basin is the hardest method of training. In it the legs are bent as much as possible, with the heel, buttocks and knee forming a triangle. The centre of gravity of the whole body settles on the legs, and walking is performed as slowly as possible.

三盘的练法以中盘练法最相宜。现在全国练习八卦掌的都是炼中盘，惟有练习单架子的时候，才炼下盘功夫。

Of the three, the middle basin is the most practical for training. Nowadays most people in China train the middle basin, only using the low basin when training individual postures.

八卦掌的主要掌法
The Main Palm Techniques of Baguazhang

八卦掌的主要掌法，分为仰掌，俯掌，竖掌，抱掌，劈掌，撩掌，挑掌，螺旋掌等八种。

The main palm techniques are: supine palm, prone palm, upright palm, embracing palm, splitting palm, pulling palm, lifting palm, and spiral palm, among others.

仰掌   *yǎng zhǎng*   Supine palm
掌心向上，五指分开，掌心凹空，如图子。

The palm heart faces up, the fingers and thumb are spread, and the palm heart is concave, as in drawing 1.

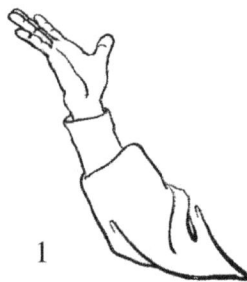

俯掌   *fǔ zhǎng*   Prone palm
掌心向下，五指分开，如图丑。

The palm heart faces down with the fingers and thumb spread, as in drawing 2.

竖掌   *shù zhǎng*   Upright palm
食指，中指，无名指，小指向上分开竖直，拇指斜向上与食指作八字形，掌心向外，手腕上屈，如图寅。

又有掌心向里或向左右者，亦叫竖掌。左右手相同。

The four fingers are spread and pointing up, with the thumb pointing obliquely up forming the Chinese numeral eight with the index finger. The palm heart faces out and the wrist is hyperflexed, as in drawing 3.

This can also be performed with the palm facing in or to the right or left, and is still called the upright palm.

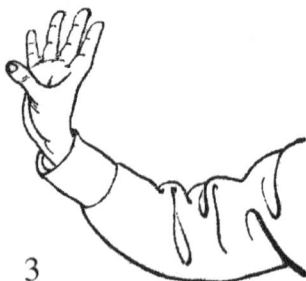

抱掌   bào zhǎng   Embracing palm

五指分开，拇指外侧向上，掌心向里，屈肘向身前作环抱式，如图卯。

The fingers and thumb are spread, with the thumb side on top and the palm heart facing in. The elbow is bent as if to hug something in front of the body, as in drawing 4.

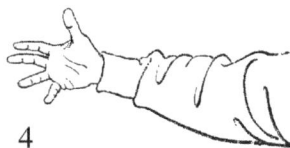

4

劈掌   pī zhǎng   Splitting palm

五指分开，拇指外侧向上，小指外侧向下，掌指向前，由上向下直劈，如图辰。

The fingers and thumb are spread with the thumb edge on top and the little finger edge below, the fingers pointing forward. The action is that of chopping directly down from above, as in drawing 5.

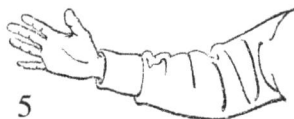

5

撩掌   liāo zhǎng   Pulling palm

五指分开，拇指外侧向上，掌心向里，由下向前撩出，如图巳。

The fingers and thumb are spread with the thumb edge on top and the palm heart facing in. The action is that of slicing forward from below, as in drawing 6.

6

挑掌   tiǎo zhǎng   Lifting palm

五指分开，由下向前，向上挑出，掌指向上，如图午。

The fingers and thumb are spread with the fingers pointing up. The action is that of lifting or scooping forward and up from below, as in drawing 7.

7

螺旋掌   luó xuán zhǎng   Spiral palm

五指分开，向前，向上臂外旋上举，小指外侧对向面部，掌心向外，
掌指向上，如图未。

The fingers and thumb are spread and raised with
the arm laterally rotated, so that the fingers point up,
the little finger edge faces the face and the palm
heart faces out, as in drawing 8.

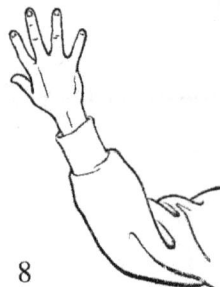

8

Part Two
八卦掌的动作解说
Description of the Eight Changes of Baguazhang

第一掌
The First Palm Change

1.1   预备式   yù bèi shì

Preparatory Stance

沿着圆圈北端开步站立，面向西方；两臂在两腿侧自然下垂，两手小指外侧贴靠两腿，手心向前；两眼平视。

Stand at the North pole of a circle, facing West, standing upright with the feet in an open stance. Hold the arms naturally by the sides with the little fingers touching the legs and the palms facing forward. Look straight ahead. (images 1.1, and photo from the side)

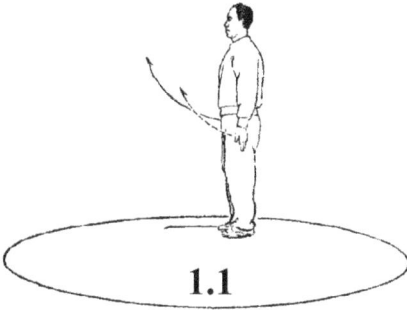

1.1

1.1

1.1 from side

注：图中表示动作趋向的箭头是：左手左脚用虚线，右手右脚用实线。

Note: In the drawings, the left hand and foot are indicated by a dotted line and the right hand and foot by a solid line.

15

要点：头往上顶，项要竖直，全身放松；两脚开步的中间距离，与两肩宽。

Pointers: Press the head up with the neck straight and the body relaxed. Stand with the feet shoulder width apart.

Translator's note: Some take the direction as an absolute direction to be used for regular training. Some take this direction as a convenience for the sake of describing the movements. Most people start with the heels together. If the left foot is not turned out at this point, it needs to turn at the beginning of the following move.

1.2   倚马问路   yǐ mǎ wèn lù

Leaning On A Horse To Ask The Way

右足向前迈进一步，足尖里扣，同时两手由下向前上斜形伸出，手心向上成仰掌，右手在前，左手在后；两肘屈成半圆形，眼平看右掌。

Step forward hooking in the right foot while bringing the hands forward and up, reaching out in supine palms, the right hand in front of the left. Keep the arms curved and look at the right hand. (images 1.2)

1.2

1.2

要点：松肩松腰松胯，两腿力量平衡；右掌高不过眉，左掌在右肘里侧距离约七，八寸。

Pointers: Relax the shoulders, waist, and hip joints and keep power equally in both legs. The right hand is no higher than the eyebrows and the left hand is seven or eight inches inside the right elbow.

Translator's note: I was also taught to weight more to the rear leg, in a seventy-thirty or eighty-twenty stance with the left foot slightly turned out and the right foot aligned to the circle line. I was told to look between the hands, not to take my sightline out from the right hand.

1.3 叶底藏花   yè dǐ cáng huā

Hide A Flower Under A Leaf (right)

左足向右足前方迈进一步，足尖里扣；两腿微曲；上身右转朝向北方；右掌同时臂内旋使小指外侧向上，拇指外侧向下，屈肘环抱胸前；左掌随之向右腋下平穿，掌心向上，屈肘环抱。

Step the left foot in front of the right, hooking it inward, both legs bent. Turn the body right to face North. Medially rotate the right arm so that the little finger edge is on top and the thumb edge is under, flex the elbow to place the forearm in front of the chest as if embracing. Stab the left hand flat in under the right armpit with the palm facing up and the elbow bent. The arms form an embracing posture. (images 1.3, and from behind)

1.3

1.3

1.3 from behind

1.3 from behind

要点：头向右转，眼看右肘。

Pointers: Turn the head to the right to look at the right elbow.

1.4   鸿雁出群   hóng yàn chū qún

Swan Leaves The Flock (left)

两足原地不动，上身左转；左掌从右肘下面向身体左上方（圆圈西
南方）移转上举，与头平齐；右掌同时臂外旋，随左掌转动，置于
左肘里侧；两掌成仰掌。

Turn the body to the left without moving the feet. Lift the left palm from
under the right elbow towards the upper left side of the body (towards the
circle's South-west), to head height. Laterally rotate the right arm and
follow the left palm with the right, placing it inside the left elbow. Both
palms are now supine palms. Look at the left hand. (images 1.4a)

1.4a

1.4a

Translator's note: You may also pivot the left foot on the heel as the body
turns towards the circle, opening and setting into the hips. The foot then is
already lined up for the start of the walk.

上动不停，左掌臂内旋，向身体左方转动，成竖掌；右掌随着臂内
旋，屈肘向左肋侧下按，掌心向下；上身继续向左转动；头随着左
掌向左方扭转，眼看左掌。

Without stopping, medially rotate the left arm and turn it around to the left
of the body, forming an upright palm. Medially rotate the right arm, bending
the elbow so that the right palm presses down by the left ribs with the palm
facing down. Continue to turn the body to the left; turn the head to the left
to follow the left palm with the eyes. (images 1.4b)

1.4b   1.4b

左足尖外展，右足上步，开始从北向西，向南，向东，向北沿圆圈
行走一周，走到北方原起点如图 1.5 时，再换接下一式。

Hook out the left foot and step the right foot forward, walking around the
circle in a westerly direction, following the circle around while retaining the
position of the images 1.4b. Start the next movement on returning to the
North pole of the circle.

要点：左肩左肘极力向身体左方外展，左掌高与眉齐，右掌向下向
前推按，腰向左拧，行走速度要均匀。

Pointers: Extend the left shoulder and elbow as far as possible to the left
side of the body, with the left palm at eyebrow height. Push and press the
right palm down and forward. Twist the waist to the left. Walk at an even
pace.

Translator's note: We usually lift the inside foot and step with it first. This
later, with more emphasis, becomes one of the seventy-two hidden kicks.

1.5   紫燕抛翦   zě yàn pāo jiǎn
       Violet Swallow Tosses Its Wings (right)

右足向左足前（西方）迈进一步，两足成倒八字；左掌同时臂外旋，
使拇指外侧向上，从右臂上面向右侧推出，掌心向外；有掌伸于左
臂下面，小指外侧斜向上；两掌上下交迭，头向右转，眼看左掌。

Step the right foot in front of the left (West), forming the Chinese character
eight. Laterally rotate the left arm to turn the thumb edge up, and push to
the right over the right arm with the palm facing out. Slide the right palm
along under the left arm with the little finger edge on top; the arms cross.
Turn the head to the right, looking at the left hand. (images 1.5)

1.5

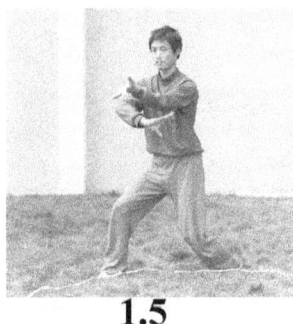

1.5

Translator's note: The larger stance in the drawing is made by stepping the left foot a bit turned out before the right step. This enables you to sit more into the left hip and step the right foot into a horse stance.

1.6   闭门推月   bì mén tuī yuè

Close The Door And Push The Moon (left)

左足向身体左侧微移，足尖外展；上身稍向左转；左掌同时臂内旋使拇指外侧向下，从右向左屈肘带回，掌心向外；右掌同时臂外旋使掌指向下，向左下方推出，掌心斜向上；眼看两掌。

Hook out the left foot to the left of the body; turn the body slightly to the left. Medially rotate the left arm to turn the thumb edge underneath, and flex the elbow to lead the hand to the left with the palm facing out. Laterally rotate the right arm so that the fingers point down and push to the lower left with the palm facing obliquely up. Look at both hands. (images 1.6)

1.6

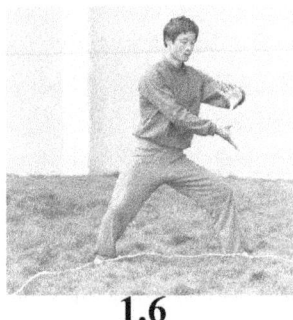

1.6

1.7   叶底藏花   yè dǐ cáng huā

Hide A Flower Under A Leaf (left)

右足向左前方迈进一步，足尖里扣；两腿微屈；上身左转朝向北方；
左掌同时稍向左带；右掌同时向左屈肘平穿，掌心向上，成仰掌。

Step the right foot out in front of the left, hooking inward. Flex the knees. Turn the body to the left towards the North. Bring the left palm slightly to the left. Stab the right palm flat out towards the left elbow with the palm facing up, forming a supine palm. (images 1.7, and from behind)

1.7

1.7

1.7 from behind

1.7 from behind

1.8   鸿雁出群   hóng yàn chū qún

Swan Leaves The Flock (right)

两足原地不动，上身右转，右掌从左肘下面向身体右上方（圆圈东
南方）移转上举，与头平齐；左掌同时臂外旋，随右掌转动，置于
右肘里侧；两掌成仰掌，眼看右掌。

Without moving the feet, turn the body to the right and lift the right palm under the left elbow up to head height at the upper right (South-east). Laterally rotate the left arm and follow the movement of the right hand with the left palm, keeping it inside the right elbow. Look at the right hand. (images 1.8a)

1.8a

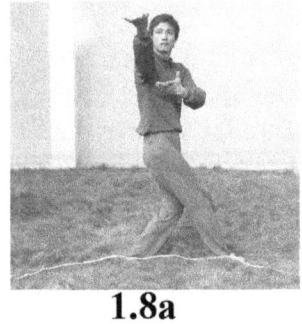

1.8a

上动不停，右掌臂内旋，向身体右方转动，成竖掌；左掌随着臂内旋，屈肘向右肋侧下按，掌心朝下；上身继续向右转动；头随着右掌向右方扭转，眼看右掌。

Medially rotate the right arm and turn it to the right of the body, forming an upright palm. Medially rotate the left arm and flex the elbow to press the palm down by the right ribs with the palm facing down. Continue to turn the body to the right. Follow the movement of the right hand with the eyes, turning the head to the right. (images 1.8b)

1.8b

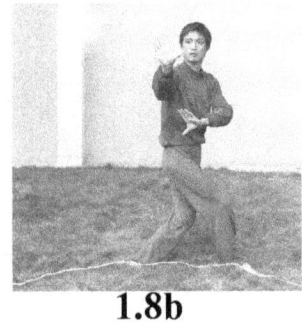

1.8b

右足尖外展，左足上步，开始从北向东，向南，向西，向北沿圆圈行走一周。走到北方原起点如图时，再换接下一式。

Hook out the right foot and step the left foot forward, starting to walk around to the circle in an easterly direction holding the same upper body position as in figure 1.8b. Go on to the next movement after completing one full circle and returning to the North pole.

1.9   紫燕抛翦   zě yàn pāo jiǎn

Violet Swallow Tosses Its Wings (left)

左足向右足前（东方）迈进一步，两足成倒八字步；右掌同时臂外旋，使拇指外侧向上，从左臂上面向左侧推出，掌心向外；左掌伸于右臂下面，小指外侧斜向上；两掌上下交迭，头向左转，眼看右掌。

Step the left foot in front of the right (East), forming the Chinese character eight 八. Laterally rotate the right arm so that the thumb edge is on top, and push out over the left arm to the left, with the palm facing out. Extend the left palm over the right arm with the little finger edge on top – the arms cross. Turn the head to the left and look at the right palm. (images 1.9)

1.9

1.9

1.10   闭门推月   bì mén tuī yuè

Close The Door And Push The Moon (right)

右足向身体右侧微移，足尖外展；上身稍向右转；右掌同时臂内旋使拇指外侧向下，从左向右屈肘带回，掌心向外；左掌同时臂外旋使掌指向下，向右下方推出，掌心斜向上；眼看两掌。

Shift the right foot slightly to the right of the body, hooking the foot out. Turn the body slightly to the right. Medially rotate the right arm to turn the thumb side down, bending the elbow to draw the hand back with the palm facing out. Laterally rotate the left arm so that the fingers point down, and push to the lower right with the palm obliquely facing up. Look at both hands. (images 1.10)

1.10

1.10

1.11　叶底藏花　　　　yè dǐ cáng huā

Hide A Flower Under A Leaf (right)

左足向右足前方迈进一步，足尖里扣；两腿微屈，上身右转朝向北方；右掌同时稍向右带；左掌同时向右屈肘平穿；掌心向上，成仰掌。

Hook in the left foot in front of the right. Keep the legs bent and turn the body to the right, towards the North. Draw the right hand slightly to the right. Flex the left elbow and stab the left palm flat to the right with the palm facing up in a supine palm.

(images 1.11)

1.11

1.11

1.12　鸿雁出群　　　　hóng yàn chū qún

Swan Leaves The Flock (left)

两足原地不动。上身左转；左掌从右肘下面向身体左上方（圆圈西南方）移转上举，与头平齐；右掌同时臂外旋，随左掌转动，置于左肘里侧；两掌成仰掌，眼看左掌。

Turn the body to the left without moving the feet. Rotate and lift the left palm from below the right elbow towards the upper left of the body (Southwest) to head height. Laterally rotate the right arm and follow the movement of the left, keeping the hand inside the left elbow. Both palms form supine palms. Look at the left hand. (images 1.12a)

1.12a

1.12a

上动不停，左掌臂内旋，向身体左方转动，成竖掌；右掌随着臂内旋，屈肘向左肋侧下按，掌心向下；上身继续向左转动；头随着左掌向左方扭转，眼看左掌。

Medially rotate the left arm and turn the hand to the left of the body forming an upright palm. Medially rotate the right arm and flex the elbow to press the palm down by the left ribs with the palm facing down. Continue to turn the body to the left. Follow the movement of the left hand with the eyes, turning the head left. (images 1.12b)

1.12b

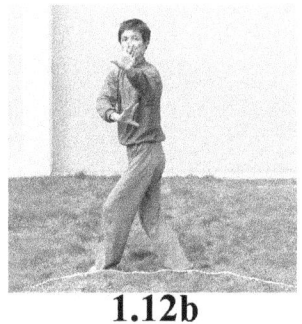

1.12b

第二掌

The Second Palm Change

左足尖外展，右足上步，开始从北向西，向南，向东，向北沿圆圈行走一周。走到北方原地点如图时，再换接下一式。

Hook out the left foot and step the right forward, starting to walk westward around the circle, holding the upper body posture of figure 1.12b. Go on to the next movement after completing a full circle and returning to the North pole.

要点：与第一掌第四动鸿雁出群同。

Pointers: Extend the left shoulder and elbow as far as possible to the left side of the body, with the left palm at eyebrow height. Push and press the right palm down and forward. Twist the waist to the left. Walk at an even pace.

Translator's note: We usually lift the left foot and step it first.

2.1   紫燕抛翦   zě yàn pāo jiǎn

Violet Swallow Tosses Its Wings (right)

右足向左前（西方）迈进一步，两足成倒八字步；左掌同时臂外旋，使拇指外侧向上，从右臂上面向右侧推出，掌心向外；右掌伸于左臂下面，小指外侧斜向上；两掌上下交迭，头向右转，眼看左掌。

Step the right foot in front of the left (West), forming the Chinese character eight 八. Laterally rotate the left arm so that the thumb edge is on top, and push to the right over the right arm with the palm facing out. Extend the right palm out under the left arm with the little finger edge on top. The arms cross. Turn the head to the right, looking at the left palm. (images 2.1)

2.1

2.1

要点：与第一掌第五动紫燕抛翼同。

Pointers: Relax the shoulders, waist, and hips. Hold the arms in front of the chest in an embracing posture – do not cross them too tightly.

Translator's note: You may also start with a *baibu* on the inside foot, then *koubu* the outside foot to a horse stance.

2.2   闭门推月   bì mén tuī yuè

Close The Door And Push The Moon (left)

左足向身体左侧微移，足尖外展，上体稍向左转；左掌同时臂内旋使拇指外侧向下，从右向左屈肘带回，掌心向外；右掌同时臂外旋使掌指向下，向左下方推出，掌心斜向上；眼看两掌。

Shift the left foot to the left of the body, pressing it outwards. Turn the body slightly to the left. Medially rotate the left arm so that the thumb is on the bottom and flex the elbow to draw the hand to the left with the palm facing out. Laterally rotate the right arm so that the fingers point down and push to the lower left with the palm facing up. Look at both hands. (images 2.2)

2.2

2.2

要点：与第一掌第六动闭门推月同。

Pointers: The arms form semi circles, they should not be too tightly bent.

2.3   猛虎出柙   měng hǔ chū xiá

Fierce Tiger Escapes From The Cage (left)

右足向左足前迈进一步，两腿微屈；上身左转；右掌同时从左臂里
面向上屈肘穿出，成螺旋掌，小指外侧对向面部；左掌同时向身前
推出，成竖掌；眼看左掌。

Step the right foot in front of the left with the knees slightly bent. Turn the
body to the left. Flex the elbow and thread the right palm out and up from
inside the left arm, forming a spiral palm with the little finger edge towards
the face. Push the left palm out in front of the body, forming an upright
palm. Look at the left hand. (images 2.3)

2.3

2.3

要点：两肩放松；右掌稍搞过头；右小臂微向前斜倾；左掌高与胸
平；左肘微屈，位于右肘里侧；两掌上下成直线。

Pointers: Relax the shoulders. The right palm is slightly higher than the
head. The right forearm is inclined slightly forward. The left palm is at chest
height. The left elbow is bent inside the right elbow. The palms are in line,
one above the other.

Translator's note: Some push with the arm quite straight and the rear leg
quite straight as well, shifting into a bow stance. Some keep the weight back
in a sixty-forty stance, and the arms more bent.

2.4   金鸡撒膀   jīn jī sā bǎng

Golden Pheasant Shakes Its Wings (left)

右掌从上由胸前屈肘下沉，叉于右腰侧，拇指在后，其余四指在前，
左足同时向西北方伸出，左腿伸直；右足尖同时里扣，右腿屈膝下
蹲；左掌随着左腿反臂伸出，掌心反向上；头随着左掌向左扭转，
上身前俯，眼看左掌。

Bend the right elbow and sink the right palm down in front of the chest,
placing it at the right waist with the thumb behind and the fingers in front.
Step the left foot to the North-west and extend the leg. Hook in the right foot
and squat on the right leg. Extend the left palm out along the left leg with

the arm rolled over, with the palm also rolled over to face up. Turn the head to follow the left palm and lean forward, looking at the left hand. (images 2.4, and from behind)

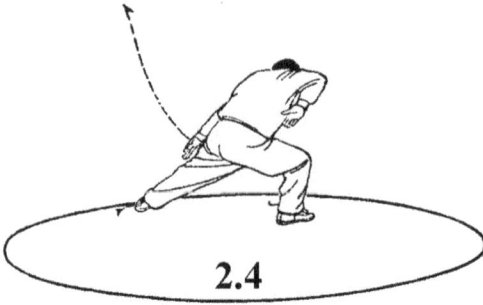

2.4

2.4

2.4 from behind

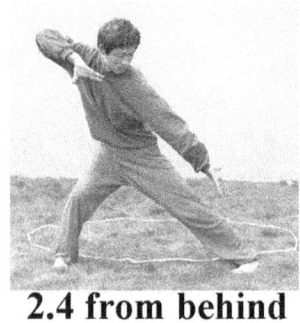

2.4 from behind

要点：全身重量在右腿，左腿作仆步。

Pointers: The weight is on the right leg, forming a left drop stance.

Translator's note: All Golden Pheasant moves are not done in a drop stance, but is a higher, more turned stance. It is a tucked in bow stance (a tucked in bow stance has the front leg bent and toed in) that puts power outward to the extending leg, into the palms, shaking into the arms with an outward force, as is shown in the drawing and the photo. If Cai Yuua is in a high stance it is because it is supposed to be like that, he is perfectly capable of dropping down. Note also that the body is turned towards the bent leg, which is a bow stance configuration. The attention is on the rear, extending, leg. This later becomes one of the seventy-two hidden kicks – a low kick to the heel or outer edge. There is another stance that is called pubu, written 铺, similar to a drop stance, but a bit higher, with the weight more between the legs. Jiang wrote in traditional characters, so perhaps the typesetter into simplified characters erroneously substituted pu 仆?

The upper hand may be at waist height, shoulder height, or higher, as long as the alignment of that arm and hand is assisting the power of the hand at the knee. The elbow must remain on line, not stick out behind.

2.5   移花接木   yí huā jiē mù

Move A Flower To Graft A Branch (left)

左足尖外展，上身直起，右腿伸直，右足随之进半步；左掌臂外旋
使掌心向上，由下向上托起，成仰掌，肘微屈；眼看左掌。

Hook out the left foot and stand up, extending the right leg and stepping forward a half step with the right foot. Laterally rotate the left arm and turn the palm up, lifting up in a supine palm with the elbow bent. Look at the left hand. (images 2.5, and photo from behind)

2.5

2.5

2.5 from behind

要点：头往上顶，项要竖直，两腿力量平
衡，左掌高与头平齐。

Pointers: Press the head up and straighten the nape of the neck. Keep power evenly in both legs. The left palm is at head height.

2.6   脑后摘盔   nǎo hòu zhāi kuī

Pick A Helmet Behind The Head (right)

右足向左足前方上步，足尖里扣，成倒八字步；身体同时左转；右
掌臂外旋使掌心向上，从右腰侧由左臂下面向左穿出；左掌位置不
变，两臂上下交迭；眼看右掌。

Hook in the right foot in front of the left, forming the Chinese character eight 八. Turn the body to the left. Laterally rotate the right arm so that the palm faces up, and thread the hand out from under the left arm to the left. The left palm does not change position, so the arms are crossed. Look at the right hand. (images 2.6a)

2.6a

2.6a

两足不动，右掌从左臂下面向右，向上斜摆上举，掌心仍向上；上
体随着右转；左掌顺势屈肘置于右肘里侧；眼看右掌。

Without moving the feet, swing the right palm up from under the left arm to
the right then lift up, with the palm still facing up. Turn the body to the
right. Flex the left elbow to keep the palm inside the right elbow. Look at the
right hand. (images 2.6b)

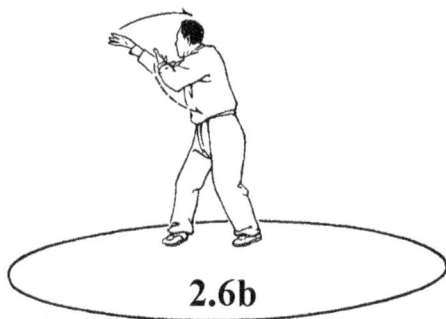

2.6b

2.6b

上动不停，右掌从右上方屈肘向脑后移转，至脑后时，向头顶上方
托起；左掌从右肘里侧落至腹前，仍为仰掌；两眼平视。

Bend the right elbow and bring the right palm down from the upper right to
behind the head. Once the hand arrives behind the head, push up above the
head. Lower the left palm from by the right elbow to in front of the
abdomen, keeping it in a supine palm. Look straight ahead. (images 2.6c)

2.6c

2.6c

要点：头往上顶，松肩松胯，两臂始终屈肘，不要直臂。

Pointers: Press the head up and relax the shoulders and hip joints. Keep the elbows bent throughout the entire move, do not straighten them.

Translator's note: Extend the arm behind fully, in a smooth action. Press the upper back to the opposite direction to drive the movement of the arm.

2.7   怀中抱月   huái zhōng bào yuè
       Embrace The Moon In The Bosom (left)

右掌从身前落下，置于右腰前，拇指向后，成俯掌；左足向左伸出，上身随着左转；左掌同时屈肘向左佣出，拇指外侧向上，掌心向里，作抱腰式；眼看左掌。

Lower the right palm in front of the body to the right waist with the thumb to the rear forming a prone palm. Extend the left foot out to the left and turn the torso to the left. Bend the left arm and press out to the left with the thumb side of the palm on top and the palm facing in, in an embracing posture. Look at the left hand. (images 2.7)

2.7

2.7

要点：两腿微屈，力量平衡，左臂要屈成平圆形，左掌与胸平齐。

Pointers: Bend the legs with the strength evenly distributed. Bend the left arm in a semi circle with the left palm at chest height.

Translator's note: The right hand braces to give balanced power to the left hand. It is usually place just off the hip. A stylistic touch is to place it on the hip bone, which is cool as long as the power flow doesn't dissipate.

2.8   叶底藏花   yè dǐ cáng huā

Hide A Flower Under A Leaf (left)

右足向左足前方迈进一步，足尖里扣；两腿微屈；上身左转朝向北方；左掌同时臂内旋使拇指外侧向下，屈肘向左平带；右掌随之臂外旋使掌心向上，向左腋下穿出。

Hook in the right foot in front of the left. Flex the knees. Turn the torso to the left, towards the North. Medially rotate the left arm to turn the thumb side down. Flex the left elbow and draw the palm across to the left. Laterally rotate the right arm to turn the palm up, and stab out under the left armpit. (images 2.8)

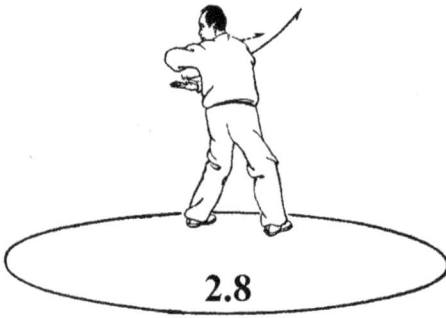

2.8

2.8

要点：与第一掌第三动叶底藏花同，唯方向相反。

Pointers: Turn the head to the left to look at the left elbow.

2.9   鸿雁出群   hóng yàn chū qún

Swan Leaves The Flock (right)

两足原地不动，上身右转；右掌从左肘下面向身体右上方（圆圈东南方）移转上举，与头平齐；左掌同时臂外旋，随右掌转动，置于右肘里侧；两掌成仰掌，眼看右掌。

Turn the body to the right without moving the feet. Rotate and lift the right palm from below the left elbow to head height at the upper right of the body (South-east). Laterally rotate the left palm and follow the movement of the right hand, keeping the hand inside the right elbow. Both palms form supine palms. Look at the right hand. (images 2.9a)

2.9a

2.9a

上动不停，右掌臂内旋，向身体右方转动，成竖掌；左掌随着臂内旋，屈肘向右肋侧下按，掌心向下；上身继续向右转动；头随着右掌向右方扭转，眼看右掌。

Medially rotate the right arm and turn to the right of the body forming an upright palm. Medially rotate the left arm and flex the elbow to press down by the right ribs with the palm facing down. Continue to turn the body to the right. Turn the head right to follow the movement of the right hand with the eyes (images 2.9b)

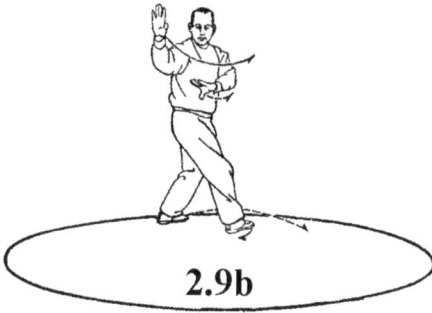

2.9b

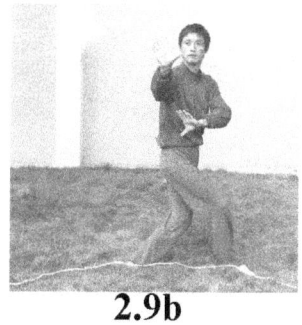

2.9b

右足尖外展，左足上步，开始从北向东，向南，向西，向北沿圆圈行走一周。走到北方远地点如图2.15时再换接下一式。

Hook out the right foot and step the left forward, starting to walk eastward around the circle holding the upper body position of images 2.9b. Start the next movement after completing a full circle and returning to the North pole of the circle.

要点：与第一掌第四动鸿雁出群同，唯方向相反。

Pointers: Pull the right shoulder and elbow around as far as possible to the right, with the right palm at eyebrow height. Push and press the left palm down and forward. Twist the waist to the right and walk at an even pace.

Translator's note: Some people pivot the right foot on the heel, opening the hip during the turn of the body. Note that in the photo Cai Yuhua has already turned his foot.

2.10 紫燕抛翦   zě yàn pāo jiǎn
Violet Swallow Tosses Its Wings (left)

左足向右足前（东方）迈进一步，两足成倒八字步；右掌同时臂外旋，使拇指外侧向上，从左臂上面向左侧推出，掌心向外；左掌伸于右臂下面，小指外侧斜向上；两掌上下交迭，头向左转，眼看右掌。

Step the left foot in front of the right (East), forming the Chinese character eight 八. Laterally rotate the right arm to turn the thumb side on top, and push to the left over the left arm with the palm facing out. Extend the left palm out under the right arm with the little finger side on top. The arms cross, one above the other. Turn the head to the left, looking at the right hand. (images 2.10)

2.10

2.10

2.11 闭门推月   bì mén tuī yuè
Close The Door And Push The Moon (right)

右足向身体右侧微移，足尖外展；上身稍向右转；右掌同时臂内旋使拇指外侧向下，从左向右屈肘带回，掌心向外；左掌同时外旋使掌指向下，向右下方推出，掌心斜向上；眼看两掌。

Hook out the right foot to the right of the body. Turn the torso slightly to the right. Medially rotate the right arm to turn the thumb to the bottom, and flex the elbow to draw the palm across to the right with the palm facing out. Laterally rotate the left arm so that the fingers point down and push to the lower right with the palm facing obliquely up. Look at both hands. (images 2.11)

2.11

2.11

2.12　猛虎出柙　　　　　měng hǔ chū xiá

Fierce Tiger Escapes From The Cage (right)

左足向右足前方迈进一步，两腿微屈；上身右转；左掌同时从右臂里面向上屈肘穿出，成螺旋掌，小指外侧对向面部；右掌同时向身前推出，成竖掌；眼看右掌。

Step the left foot in front of the right with the knees slightly bent. Turn the torso to the right. Thread the left palm out and up from inside the right arm, forming a spiral palm with the little finger edge towards the face and the elbow bent. Push the right palm out with an upright palm in front of the body. Look at the right hand. (images 2.12)

2.12

2.12

2.13　金鸡撒膀　　　　　jīn jī sā bǎng

Golden Pheasant Shakes Its Wings (right)

左掌从上由胸前屈肘下沉，叉于左腰侧，拇指在后，其余四指在前；右足同时向东北方伸出，右腿伸直；左足尖同时里扣；左腿屈膝下蹲；右掌随之顺着右腿反臂伸出，掌心反向上；头随着右掌向右扭转，上身前俯，眼看右掌。

Bend the left elbow and sink the left palm down past the chest, placing it by the left waist with the thumb behind and the fingers in front. Step the right foot to the North-east and extend the leg. Turn the left foot in and squat on the left leg. Extend the right palm out along the right leg with the arm rolled

over, rolling the palm over to face up. Turn the head right to follow the right
hand with the eyes, and lean forward. (images 2.13, and photo from behind)

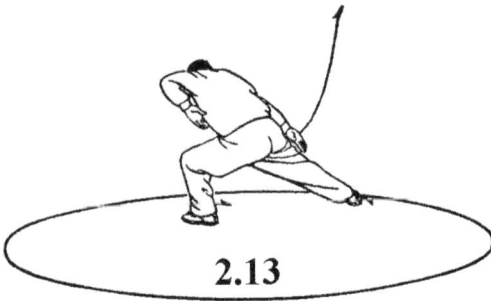

2.13

2.13

2.13 from behind

2.14   移花接木   yí huā jiē mù

Move A Flower To Graft A Branch (right)

右足尖外展，上身直起，左腿伸直，左足随之进半步；右掌臂外旋
使掌心向上，由下向上托起，成仰掌肘微屈；眼看右掌。

Hook out the right foot and straighten the body, extending the left leg and
stepping a half step with the left foot. Laterally rotate the right arm to turn
the palm up, lifting up in a supine palm with the elbow bent. Look at the
right hand. (images 2.14, and photo from behind)

2.14

2.14

2.14 from behind

2.15　脑后摘盔　　　　　nǎo hòu zhāi kuī

Pick A Helmet Behind The Head (left)

左足向右足前方上步，足尖里扣，成倒八字步；身体同时右转；左掌臂外旋使手心向上，从腰侧由右臂下面向右穿出；右掌位置不变，两臂上下交迭。

Hook in the left foot in front of the right, forming the Chinese character eight 八. Turn the body to the right. Laterally rotate the left arm to turn the palm up, and thread out to the right under the right arm. The right palm does not change position, so the arms are crossed, one above the other. (images 2.15a)

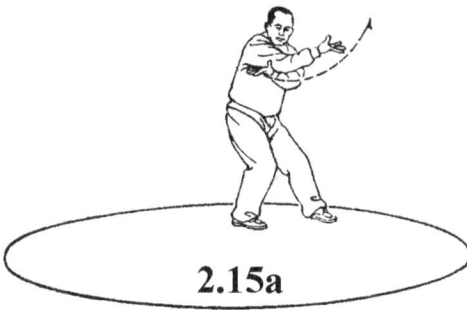

2.15a

2.15a

两足不动，左掌从右臂下面向左，向上斜摆上举，掌仍向上；上身随着左转；右掌顺势屈肘置于左肘里侧；眼看左掌。

Without moving the feet, swing the left palm up from under the right arm to the left and up, with the palm still facing up. Turn the body to the left. Flex the right elbow to keep the palm inside the left elbow. Look at the left hand. (images 2.15b)

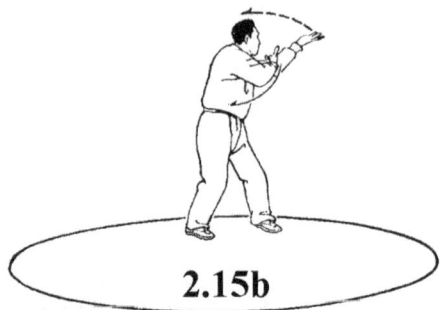

2.15b

2.15b

上动不停，左掌从左上方屈肘向脑后移转；至胸后时，向头顶上方托起；右掌从左肘里侧落至腹前，仍为仰掌；两眼平视。

Bend the left elbow, bringing the palm down behind the head from the upper left. Once it gets behind the head, push up above the head. Lower the right palm past the left elbow to in front of the abdomen, keeping it in a supine palm. Look straight ahead. (images 2.15c)

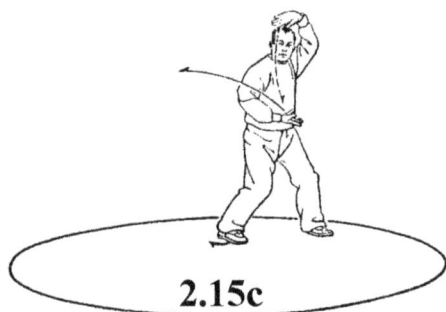

2.15c

2.15c

2.16   怀中抱月   huái zhōng bào yuè

Embrace The Moon In The Bosom (right)

左掌从身前落下，置于左腰前，拇指向后，成俯掌；右足向右伸出，上身随之右转；右掌同时屈肘向右俪出，拇指外侧向上，掌心向里作抱腰式；眼看右掌。

Lower the left palm in front of the body to place it by the left waist in a prone palm with the thumb to the rear. Extend the right foot out to the right and turn the torso to the right. Flex the right elbow and press out to the right with the thumb side on top and the palm facing in, in an embracing posture. Look at the right hand. (images 2.16)

2.16

2.16

2.17 叶底藏花   yè dǐ cáng huā

Hide A Flower Under A Leaf (right)

左足向右足前迈进一步，足尖里扣；两腿微屈；上身右转朝向北方；
右掌同时臂内旋使拇指外侧向下，屈肘向右平带；左掌随之臂外旋
使掌心向上，向右腋下穿出。

Hook in the left foot in front of the right. Slightly flex both knees. Turn the body right to face the North. Medially rotate the right arm so that the thumb side is on bottom and flex the elbow to draw the palm across to the right. Laterally rotate the left palm and stab the left hand in under the right armpit with the palm facing up. (images 2.17)

2.17

2.17

要点：与第一掌第三动叶底藏花同。

Pointers: Turn the head to the right to look at the right elbow.

2.18 鸿雁出群   hóng yàn chū qún

Swan Leaves The Flock (left)

两足原地不动，上身左转；左掌从右肘下面向身体左上方（圆圈西
南方）移转上举，与头平齐；右掌同时臂外旋，随左掌转动，置于
左肘里侧；两掌成仰掌，眼看左掌。

Turn the body to the left without moving the feet. Turn and lift the left palm
from under the right elbow to head height at the upper left side of the body
(towards the South-west). Laterally rotate the right arm and turn with the
left hand, keeping the hand on the inside of the left elbow. Both palms are
supine palms. Look at the left hand. (images 2.18a)

2.18a

2.18a

上动不停，左掌臂内旋，向身体左方转动，成竖掌；右掌随着臂内
旋，屈肘向左侧下按，掌心向下；上身继续向左转动；头随着左掌
向左方扭转，眼看左掌。

Medially rotate the left arm and bring the hand around to the left of the
body, forming an upright palm. Medially rotate the right arm, flex the elbow
and press the right palm down by the left side with the palm facing down.
Continue to turn the body to the left. Follow the leftward movement of the
hands with the head, looking at the left hand. (images 2.18b)

2.18b

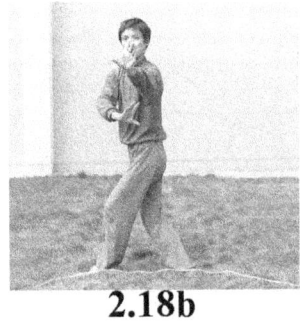

2.18b

第三掌

The Third Palm Change

左足尖外展，右足上步，开始从北向西，向南，向东，向北沿圆圈行走一周。走到北方原起点如图时，再换接下一式。

Hook out the left foot and step forward with the right foot, starting to walk around the circle in a westerly direction with the upper body posture taken in the images 2.18b, then following the circle around. Begin the next movement on returning to the North pole of the circle.

要点：与第一掌第四动鸿雁出群同。

Pointers: Turn the left shoulder and elbow are far as possible around to the left, with the left palm at eyebrow height. Push and press the right palm down and forward. Twist the waist to the left and walk at an even pace.

3.1 紫燕抛翦   zě yàn pāo jiǎn

Violet Swallow Tosses Its Wings (right)

右足向左足前（西方）迈进一步，两足成倒八字步；左掌同时臂外旋，使拇指外侧向上，从右臂上面向右侧推出，掌心向外；右掌伸于左臂下面，小指外侧斜向上；两掌上下交迭；头向右转，眼看左掌。

Step the right foot in front of the left (West), forming the Chinese character eight 八. Laterally rotate the left arm so that the thumb edge turns up, and push to the right over the right arm with the palm facing out. Extend the right palm along under the left arm with the little finger edge on top. The arms cross, one above the other. Turn the head right to look at the left hand. (images 3.1)

43

3.1

3.1

要点：与第一掌第五动紫燕抛翦同。

Pointers: Relax the shoulders, waist, and hips. Hold the arms in front of the chest in an embracing posture – do not cross them too tightly.

Translator's note: Again, this can start with the inside foot turned out, then a be a larger tucked in step into a horse stance.

3.2   闭门推月   bì mén tuī yuè

   Close The Door And Push The Moon (left)

左足向身体左侧微移，组建外展；上身稍向左转；左掌同时臂外旋使拇指外侧向下，从右向左屈肘带回，掌心向外；右掌同时臂外旋使掌指向下，向左下方推出，掌心斜向上；眼看两掌。

Shift the left foot to the left of the body, hooking out. Turn the body slightly to the left. Laterally rotate the left arm so that the thumb is on the bottom. Flex the left elbow to draw the palm across to the left with the palm facing out. Laterally rotate the right arm to point the fingers down, and push to the lower left with the palm facing up. Look at both hands. (images 3.2)

3.2

3.2

要点：与第一掌第六动闭门推月同。

Pointers: The arms form semi circles – they should not be too tightly bent.

3.3   鹞子钻天   yào zǐ zuān tiān

Sparrow Hawk Pierces The Sky (right)

右足向左足前迈进一步，两足成倒八字步；身体随着左转；右掌同
时从左臂外面向上举起，掌背向外；左掌随之向裆前落下，掌心向
外；眼看右掌。

Step the right foot in front of the left, forming the Chinese character eight 八
and turning the body left. Lift the right palm up along the outside of the left
arm with the back of the hand facing out. Lower the left palm to in front of
the groin with the palm facing out. Look at the right hand. (images 3.3 and
from behind)

3.3

3.3

3.3 from behind

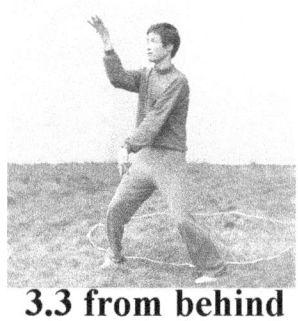

3.3 from behind

要点：两腿弯曲，两膝里扣，右掌上举离头顶约七，八寸。

Pointers: The knees are bent and turned in. The right hand is seven or eight
inches above the head.

Translator's note: The lower palm maintains a power of pushing away from
yourself. The upper wrist is straight, putting power to the fingertips.

3.4   白蛇缠身   bái shé chán shēn

White Snake Coils Its Body (right)

两足原地不动，右掌在头顶上方从右向前，向左，向后划一小圆圈，右臂随着内旋，掌心向上成托掌；身体同时左转；左掌随之由裆前贴着左胯绕向背后屈肘，掌心向外；眼看左肩。

Without moving the feet, describe a small circle with the right palm above the head to the front, left, then back, then medially rotate the right arm to push up with the palm. Turn the body to the left. Flex the left elbow slightly and slide the palm around the left hip to behind the body with the palm turned out. Look at the left shoulder. (images 3.4)

3.4

3.4

要点：拧腰，松胯，两臂均屈。

Pointers: Twist the waist. Relax the hips. Bend the arms.

3.5   怀中抱月   huái zhōng bào yuè

Embrace The Moon In The Bosom (left)

左足从身后向右侧撤一步，上身随着从左向后转，右足尖里扣，两腿均屈膝略蹲；右掌同时从上由胸前落下，置于右腰侧，拇指向后，成俯掌；左掌随之从背后绕向身前，臂外旋使拇指外侧向上，掌心向里，作抱腰式；眼看左掌。

Step the left foot around to the right of the body, then turn the torso to the right, hooking the right foot in and bending the knees. Lower the right palm past the chest and place it by the right waist in a prone palm with the thumb to the rear. Coil the left palm around the body from the back to the front and laterally rotate so that the thumb is on top with the palm facing in, in an embracing posture. Look at the left hand. (images 3.5)

3.5

3.5

要点：两腿微屈，力量平衡，左臂要屈成平圆形，左掌与胸平齐。

Pointers: Bend the legs with the strength evenly distributed. Bend the left arm in a semi circle with the left palm at chest height.

3.6　玉女献书　　　　yǔ nǚ xiàn shū

Beautiful Girl Presents A Book (right)

右足向左足前迈进半部；右掌同时从左臂下面向前屈肘穿出，掌心向上；左掌随之臂内旋使小指外侧向上，从右臂上面屈肘收于右肩外侧；眼看右掌。

Step the right foot a half step in front of the left. Stab the right palm out along under the left arm to the front with the elbow bent and the palm facing up. Medially rotate the left palm to turn the little finger edge up, and flex the elbow to bring the hand in along top the right arm to outside the right shoulder. Look at the right hand. (images 3.6)

3.6

3.6

要点：两腿微屈，松肩沉肘，右掌高于眉齐。

Pointers: Bend the knees, relax the shoulders, and sink the elbows. The right palm is at eyebrow height.

Translator's note: The drawing has the thumb tucked into the elbow crease, palm angled forward and up. The photo has the little finger tucked into the elbow crease, palm facing up, as learned by Cai Yuhua. The hand is always placed at the elbow crease, and usually the thumb is tucked into it, which turns the palm forward. Different branches of the style are quite specific about whether the palm is up or down.

3.7　泰山压顶　　　　tài shān yā dǐng

Mount Tai Bears Down Its Weight (right)

右足尖里扣，左足尖外展，上身左转向西；右掌同时从右向后转至头顶上方，掌心仍向上；左掌随之从右肩外侧落至腹前，掌心向上；眼向西方平视。

Hook in the right foot then hook out the left foot. Turn the body left to face West. Turn the right palm back above the head with the palm still facing up. Lower the left palm in front of the abdomen with the palm facing up. Look to the West. (images 3.7)

要点：两腿力量腰平衡，右掌离头顶约四，五寸。

Pointers: The strength of the legs is evenly distributed. The right hand is four or five inches above the head.

Translator's note: The right hand pushes up over the head at the first part of the turn. In the photo, Cai Yuhua has already turned further, as the hand is starting to push down.

3.8　黑熊反背　　　　hēi xióng fǎn bèi

Black Bear Rolls Over (left)

右足向左足前迈进一步，上身左转向南，两腿屈膝成马步；右掌同时从身前向右侧下按，掌心向下；左掌同时由腹前向左侧下按，掌心向下；两臂均微屈；眼看左掌。

Step the right foot in front of the left, turning the torso left to face South, the legs bent to form a horse stance. Press the right palm down the front of the body to the right side with the palm facing down. Press the left palm down to the left side with the palm facing down. Keep both arms slightly bent. Look at the left hand. (images 3.8)

3.8

3.8

要点：两腿稍屈，松腰松胯。

Pointers: Keep the knees slightly bent. Relax the lumbar area and waist, and relax the hip joints.

Translator's note: The brace may also be done more out than down, at almost shoulder height.

3.9 黄鹰掐脖   huáng yīng qiā bó

Yellow Eagle Clutches The Throat (right)

左足尖外展，右足尖里扣，上身左转；左掌同时在身前提起，右掌则从左掌下面向身前屈肘伸出，掌指向上，掌心朝前；左掌在右掌伸出后，屈肘落于左腰侧，掌指向前，掌心向下；眼看右掌。

Hook the left foot out and the right foot in, turning the torso to the left. Raise the left palm in front of the body, then extend the right palm out under the left hand in front of the body with the fingers pointing up and the palm facing forward. After the right palm pushes out, flex the left elbow to bring the left palm in by the left waist with the fingers pointing forward and the palm facing down. Look at the right hand. (drawing 3.9 and photo 3.9a)

Photo 3.9b is doing the grab to the following move.

3.9

3.9a

要点：右掌高于眉齐，两臂均屈，沉肩坠肘。

Pointers: The right hand is at eyebrow height and the arms are bent. Sink the shoulders and elbows.

3.9b

Translator's note: Some branches go into a full bow stance with a straight rear leg, some go into more of a crouch, or dragon riding, stance. Similarly, the reaching arm may be quite extended or not. Some do it as a push, as in the drawing. Some do this with the tiger's mouth on top, the fingers turned to the side, and the palm partly closed, as in the photo 3.9a, as if grabbing the throat. In some branches there is a following transitional move of close, twist, and pop up, to grab and break the windpipe, as shown in photo 3.9b.

3.10 黄鹰掐脖   huáng yīng qiā bó

Yellow Eagle Clutches The Throat (left)

右足向左足前迈进一步，两腿微屈；左掌同时从右掌下面屈肘向身前伸出，掌指向上，掌心向前；右掌同时屈肘收于由腰侧，掌指向前，掌心向下；眼看左掌。

Step the right foot in front of the left with the legs bent. Extend the left hand out underneath the right palm with the fingers pointing up and the palm facing forward. Bring the right hand back to the right waist with the fingers pointing forward and the palm facing down. Look at the left hand. (images 3.10)

3.10

3.10

要点：左掌高于眉齐，两臂均屈，沉肩坠肘。

Pointers: The left hand is at eyebrow height and the arms are bent. Sink the shoulders and elbows.

3.11 猿猴摘果   yuán hóu zhāi guǒ

Ape Picks Fruit (left)

右足尖里扣，左足尖外展，上身随着从左向后转，面向西北；左掌同时将无名指和小指屈拢，用拇指压住，食指和中指伸直，从身前落下，向后屈肘伸出，掌心向上；右掌不变，随身转动；眼看左掌。

Hook the right foot in and the left foot out, turn the body to the back so that it faces North-west. Tuck in the ring and little fingers of the left hand, pressing them into the palm with the thumb, and extend the index and middle fingers together. Drop the left hand down in front of the body then extend it out to the back with the palm facing up. Do not move the right hand. Look at the left hand. (images 3.11)

要点：头往上顶，两肩放松，左掌高于头齐。

Pointers: Lift the head and relax the shoulders. The left hand is at head height.

3.12 猿猴坐洞   yuán hóu zuò dòng

Ape Sits In Its Cave (left)

左足退回半步，以足尖点地，右腿屈膝半蹲，成鸡登步；左掌同时收回，停于左肩旁，眼看左掌。

Bring the left foot in a half step, placing the toes on the ground. Squat on the right leg to form a chicken tread stance. Bring in the left palm to beside the left shoulder. Look at the left hand. (images 3.12)

3.12

3.12

要点：右腿支持身体重量，上身略向前倾，防止耸肩供背。

Pointers: The weight is on the right leg. Lean forward slightly. Do not shrug the shoulders or hunch the back.

3.13 麒麟吐书   qí lín tǔ shū

Kylin Tells A Story (right)

左足向西上半部，右足继之前进一步；左足提起，贴于右腿里侧，成独立步；右掌同时从左臂下面向前上穿，掌心向上，肘微屈；左掌同时将无名指，小指，拇指松开，臂内旋使掌心向下，从前向下，向后屈肘收回，置于左腰后侧；眼看右掌。

Step the left foot a half step to the West then step the right foot forward. Lift the left knee and tuck the foot in by the right leg, forming a one legged stance. Thread the right palm along under the left arm to stab to the upper front, with the palm facing up and the elbow slightly bent. Open the left hand and medially rotate the arm and flex the elbow to bring the hand down and back to behind the left waist with the palm facing down. Look at the right hand. (images 3.13)

3.13

3.13

要点：右腿微屈，头往上顶，松肩，右掌高于头齐。

Pointers: The right leg is slightly bent. Raise the head and relax the shoulders. The right hand is at head height.

Translator's note: First stab with the left hand as the left foot steps. Then cover with the left and and thread the right hand up as the right foot steps. Complete the right stab with the lifting of the left knee. The lifted foot is not pointed, the power in the lift stays in the knee.

3.14 飞燕抄水   fēi yàn chāo shuǐ

Flying Swallow Skims Over The Water (left)

左足向身后落步伸出，足尖里扣；右足尖同时里扣，右腿屈膝下蹲，成仆步；右掌同时臂内旋使掌背向下，反臂伸直；左掌则随着左腿反臂伸出，掌心反向上；上体前俯，头向左扭转，眼看左掌。

Land the left foot extended out behind the body with the foot hooked in. Turn the right foot in and squat on the right leg, forming a drop stance. Medially rotate the right arm to face the palm up, rolling the arm over and extending it. Roll the left arm over and slide the hand along the leg with the palm rolled over to face up. Lean forward and turn the head to the left, looking at the left hand. (images 3.14)

3.14

3.14

要点：全身重量，落于两腿之间，右腿尽量下蹲。

Pointers: The weight is between the legs – squat as deeply as possible.

Translator's note: The Flying Swallow is a full drop stance, so the weight is more to the squatting leg. All the Flying Swallow moves are full drop stances, while all the Golden Pheasant moves are tucked in bow stances. The body turn and the power through the arms for each move is appropriate for each stance. See my notes with move 2.4.

3.15 怀中抱月   huái zhōng bào yuè
Embrace The Moon In The Bosom (left)

上身直起，左足尖外展，右足尖里扣，两腿微屈；右掌屈肘置于右腰侧，拇指向后成俯掌；左掌同时臂外旋使拇指外侧向上，屈肘作抱腰式；眼看左掌。

Straighten the body, hook the left foot out and the right foot in, and bend the legs slightly. Flex the right elbow to bring the hand in by the right waist with the thumb behind in a prone palm. Laterally rotate the left arm to turn the thumb side up, flex the elbow in an embracing position. Look at the left hand. (images 3.15)

3.15

3.15

要点：与第二掌第九动怀中抱月同。

Pointers: Bend the legs with the strength evenly distributed. Bend the left arm in a semi circle with the left palm at chest height.

3.16 叶底藏花   yè dǐ cáng huā
Hide A Flower Under A Leaf (left)

右足向左足前方迈进一步，足尖里扣；两腿微屈；上身左转朝上北方；左掌同时臂内旋使拇指外侧向下，屈肘向左平带；右掌随着臂外旋使掌心向上，向左腋下穿出。

Hook in the right foot in front of the left. Slightly bend both legs. Turn the body left to face North. Medially rotate the left arm so that the thumb edge is underneath and flex the elbow to draw the palm across to the left. Laterally rotate the right palm and stab the hand in under the left armpit with the palm facing up. (images 3.16)

3.16

3.16

3.17　鸿雁出群　　　　　　hóng yàn chū qún

Swan Leaves The Flock (right)

两足原地不动，上身右转；右掌从左肘下面向身体右上方（圆圈东南方）移转上举，与头平齐；左掌同时臂外旋，随右掌转动，置于右肘里侧；两掌成仰掌，眼看右掌。

Turn the body to the right without moving the feet. Turn and lift the right palm from under the left elbow to head height at the upper right side of the body (towards the South-east). Laterally rotate the left arm and bring it around with the right, keeping the palm on the inside of the right elbow. Both palms are supine palms. Look at the right hand. (images 3.17a)

3.17a

3.17a

上动不停，右掌臂内旋，向身体右方转动，成竖掌；左掌随着臂内旋，屈肘向右肋侧下按，掌心向下；上身继续向右转动；头随着右掌向右方扭转，眼看右掌。

Medially rotate the right arm and bring it around to the right of the body, forming an upright palm. Medially rotate the left arm, bending the elbow to press the hand down by the right side with the palm facing down. Continue to turn the body to the right. Follow the rightward movement with the head, looking at the right hand. (images 3.17b)

3.17b

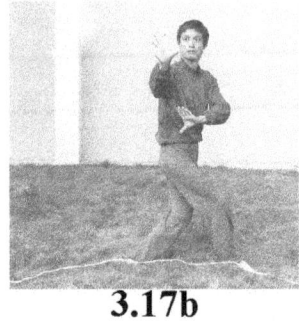

3.17b

右足尖外展，左足上步，开始从北向东，向南，向西，向北沿圆圈行走一周。走到北方远地点如图 3.21 时再换接下一式。

Hook out the right foot and step the left foot forward, starting to walk around the circle in a easterly direction. Follow the circle around holding the same position as that of images 3.17b, then begin the next movement on returning to the North pole of the circle.

要点：与第一掌第四动鸿雁出群同，唯方向相反。

Pointers: Extend the right shoulder and elbow as far as possible around to the right, with the right palm at eyebrow height. Push and press the left palm down and forward. Twist the waist to the right. Walk at an even pace.

3.18 紫燕抛翦   zě yàn pāo jiǎn

Violet Swallow Tosses Its Wings (right)

左足向右足前（东方）迈进一步，两足成倒八字步；右掌同时臂外旋，使拇指外侧向上，从左臂上面向左侧推出，掌心向外；左掌伸于右臂下面，小指外侧斜向上；两掌上下交迭，头向左转，眼看右掌。

Step the left foot in front of the right to the East, forming the Chinese character eight. Laterally rotate the right arm to turn the thumb edge up, and push to the left over the left arm with the palm facing out. Extend the left palm along under the right arm with the little finger edge on top. The arms cross, one above the other. Turn the head to the left, looking at the right palm. (images 3.18)

3.18

3.18

3.19　闭门推月　　　　bì mén tuī yuè

Close The Door And Push The Moon (right)

右足向身体右侧微移，足尖外展；上身稍向右转；右掌同时臂内旋使拇指外侧向下，从左向右屈肘带回，掌心向外；左掌同时臂外旋使掌指向下，向右下方推出，掌心斜向上；眼看两掌。

Hook out the right foot to the right of the body. Turn the body slightly to the right. Laterally rotate the right arm so that the thumb edge is on the underneath, and flex the elbow to bring the palm across to the right with the palm facing out. Laterally rotate the left arm so that the fingers point down and push to the lower right with the palm facing up. Look at both hands. (images 3.19)

3.19

3.19

3.20　鹞子钻天　　　　yào zǐ zuān tiān

Sparrow Hawk Pierces The Sky (left)

左足向右足前迈进一步，两足成倒八字步；身体随着右转；左掌同时从右臂外面向上举起，掌背向外；右掌随之向裆前落下，掌心向外；眼看左掌。

Hook in the left foot in front of the right, forming the Chinese character eight 八. Turn the body right. Lift the left palm up along the outside of the right arm with the back of the hand facing out. Lower the right palm in front of the groin with the palm facing out. Look at the left hand (images 3.20 and from behind)

3.20

3.20

3.20 from behind

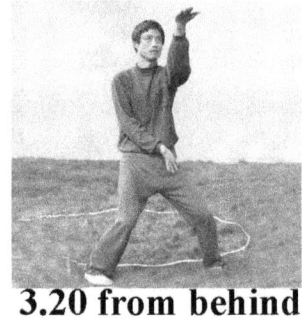

3.20 from behind

Translator's note: Another way to do this move is to push up, instead of reaching up with the wrist straight. You can see this time that Cai Yuhua's upper wrist is bent to push up, and that is how I originally learned the move.

3.21   白蛇缠身   bái shé chán shēn

White Snake Coils Its Body (left)

两足原地不动，左掌在头顶上方从左向前，向右，向后划一小圆圈，左臂随着内旋，掌心向上成托掌；身体同时右转；右掌随之由裆前贴着右胯绕向背后屈肘，掌心向外；眼看右肩。

Without moving the feet, describe a small circle to the front, right, then back with the left palm, then medially rotate the left arm to push up with the palm facing up. Turn the body to the right. Flex the right elbow and slide the right hand around the right hip and behind the body with the palm turned out. Look at the right shoulder. (images 3.21)

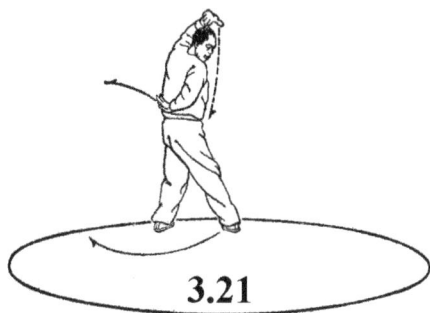

3.21

3.21

3.22   怀中抱月   huái zhōng bào yuè

Embrace The Moon In The Bosom (right)

左掌从身前落下，置于左腰前，拇指向后，成俯掌；右足向右伸出，
上身随之右转；右掌同时屈肘向右俑出，拇指外侧向上，掌心向里
作抱腰式；眼看右掌。

Step the right foot around the body to the left side, turning the body around
to the back, hooking in the left foot and bending the knees. Lower the left
palm in front of the chest to place it by the left waist in a prone palm with
the thumb to the rear. Coil the right palm around the body from the back to
the front and laterally rotate the arm so that the thumb is on top with the
palm facing in, in an embracing posture. Look at the right hand. (images
3.22)

3.22

3.22

3.23   玉女献书   yù nǚ xiàn shū

Beautiful Girl Presents A Book (left)

左足向右足前迈进半部；左掌同时从右臂下面向前屈肘穿出，掌心
向上；右掌随之臂内旋使小指外侧向上，从左臂上面屈肘收于左肩
外侧；眼看左掌。

Step the left foot a half step in front of the right. Thread the left palm along under the right arm to stab to the front with the elbow bent and the palm facing up. Medially rotate the right arm to turn the little finger side up, and flex the elbow to bring the hand along the top of the left arm to outside the left shoulder. Look at the left hand. (images 3.23)

3.23

3.23

3.24   泰山压顶   tài shān yā dǐng

Mount Tai Bears Down Its Weight (left)

左足尖里扣，右足尖外展，上身右转向东；左掌同时从左向后转至头顶上方，掌心仍向上；右掌随之从左肩外侧落至腹前，掌心向上；眼向东方平视。

Hook the left foot in and the right foot out, turn the body right to face East. Push the left palm back and up above the head with the palm facing up. Lower the right palm in front of the abdomen with the palm facing up. Look East. (images 3.24)

3.24

3.24

3.25 黑熊反背   hēi xióng fǎn bèi

Black Bear Rolls Over (right)

左足向右足前迈进一步，上身右转向南，两腿屈膝成马步；左掌同时从身前向左侧下按，掌心向下；右掌同时由腹前向右侧下按，掌心向下；两臂均微屈；眼看右掌。

Step the left foot in front of the right, turning the body right to face South, the legs bent to form a horse stance. Press the left palm down across the body to the left side with the palm facing down. Press the right palm down by the right side with the palm facing down. Keep both arms slightly bent. Look at the right hand. (images 3.25)

3.25

3.25

3.26 黄鹰掐脖   huáng yīng qiā bó

Yellow Eagle Clutches The Throat (left)

右足尖外展，左足尖里扣，上身右转；右掌同时在身前提起，左掌则从右掌下面向身前屈肘伸出，掌指向上，掌心朝前；右掌在左掌伸出后，屈肘落于右腰侧，掌指向前，掌心向下；眼看左掌。

Hook the right foot out and the left foot in. Turn the body to the right. Raise the right hand in front of the body, then extend the left palm along under the right arm in front of the body with the fingers pointing up and the palm facing forward. After the left palm extends, flex the right elbow to bring the right hand in by the right waist with the fingers pointing forward and the palm facing down. Look at the left hand. (images 3.26)

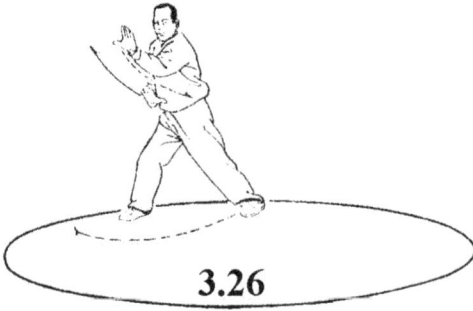

3.26

3.26

3.27 黄鹰掐脖   huáng yīng qiā bó

Yellow Eagle Clutches The Throat (right)

左足向右足前迈进一步，两腿微屈；右掌同时从左掌下面屈肘向身前伸出，掌指向上，掌心朝前；左掌同时屈肘落于左腰侧，掌指向前，掌心向下；眼看右掌。

Step the left foot in front of the right with the knees bent. Extend the right hand out below the left palm with the fingers pointing up and the palm facing forward. Bring the left palm back by the left waist with the fingers pointing forward and the palm facing down. Look at the right hand. (images 3.27)

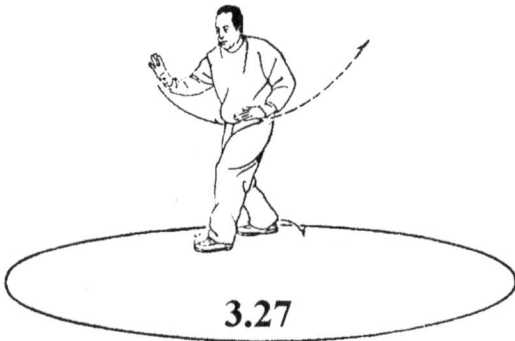

3.27

3.27

3.28 猿猴摘果   yuán hóu zhāi guǒ

Ape Picks Fruit (right)

左足尖里扣，右足尖外展，上身随着从右向后转，面向东北；右掌同时将无名指和小指屈拢，用拇指压住，食指和中指伸直，从身前落下，向后屈肘伸出，掌心向上；左掌不变，随身转动；眼看右掌。

Hook the left foot in and the right foot out, turn the body around to the back to face North-east. Tuck in the ring and little fingers of the right hand, pressing them in with the thumb, and extend the index and middle fingers. Drop the right hand down in front of the body then extend it out to the back with the palm facing up. Turn the left hand with the body, keeping in the same relative position. Look at the right hand. (images 3.28)

3.28

3.28

3.29   猿猴坐洞   yuán hóu zuò dòng

Ape Sits In Its Cave (right)

右足退回半步，以足尖点地，左腿屈膝半蹲，成鸡登步；右掌同时收回，停于右肩旁，眼看右掌。

Bring the right foot a half step back, placing the toes on the ground. Squat on the left leg to form a chicken tread stance. Bring in the right hand to beside the right shoulder. Look at the right hand. (images 3.29)

3.29

3.29

3.30 麒麟吐书　　　qí lín tǔ shū

Kylin Tells A Story (left)

右足向东上半部，左足继之前进一步；右足提起，贴于左腿里侧，
成独立步；左掌同时从右臂下面向前上穿，掌心向上，肘微屈；右
掌同时将无名指，小指，拇指松开，臂内旋使掌心向下，从前向下，
向后屈肘收回，置于右腰后侧；眼看左掌。

Step the right foot a half step to the East then step the left foot forward. Lift
the right knee and tuck the foot in by the left leg, forming a one legged
stance. Thread the left palm under the right arm to stab to the upper front,
with the palm facing up and the elbow slightly bent. Open the fingers of the
right hand and medially rotate the arm and flex the elbow to pull the hand
down and back behind the right waist with the palm facing down. Look at
the left hand. (images 3.30)

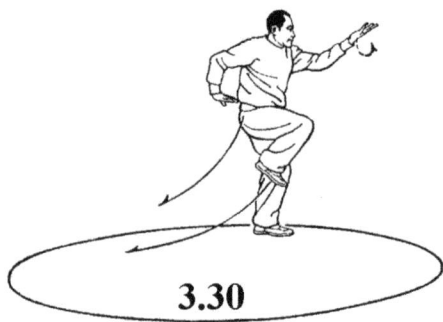

3.30

3.30

3.31 飞燕抄水　　　fēi yàn chāo shuǐ

Flying Swallow Skims Over The Water (right)

右足向身后落步伸出，足尖里扣；左足尖同时里扣，左腿屈膝下蹲，
成仆步；左掌同时臂内旋使掌背向下，反臂伸直；右掌则随着右腿
反臂伸出，掌心反向上；上体前俯，头向右扭转，眼看右掌。

Land with the right foot extended out behind the body with the foot hooked
in. Turn the left foot in and squat on the left leg, forming a drop stance.
Medially rotate the left arm to face the palm up, turning the arm over and
extending it. Roll the right arm over and slide the hand along the leg with
the palm facing up. Lean forward and turn the head right, looking at the
right hand. (images 3.31)

3.31

3.31

3.32 怀中抱月   huái zhōng bào yuè

Embrace The Moon In The Bosom (right)

上身直起，右足外展，左足尖里扣，两腿微屈；左掌屈肘置于左腰侧，拇指向后成俯掌；右掌同时臂外旋使拇指外侧向上，屈肘作抱腰式；眼看右掌。

Straighten the body, turn the right foot out and the left foot in, and flex the knees slightly. Flex the left elbow to bring the hand in by the left waist in a prone palm with the thumb behind. Laterally rotate the right arm to turn the thumb side up, flex the elbow in an embracing position. Look at the right hand. (images 3.32)

3.32

3.32

3.33 叶底藏花   yè dǐ cáng huā

Hide A Flower Under A Leaf (right)

左足向右足前方迈进一步，足尖里扣；两腿微曲；上身右转朝向北方；右掌同时臂内旋使母指外侧向下，屈肘向右平带；左掌随之臂外旋使掌心向上，向右腋下穿出。

Hook in the left foot, stepping in front of the right. Flex the knees. Turn the body right to face North. Medially rotate the right arm (so that the little finger side is on top and the thumb side is underneath) and flex the elbow to draw the hand to the right. Laterally rotate the left arm and stab the hand in under the right armpit (palm facing up). (images 3.33)

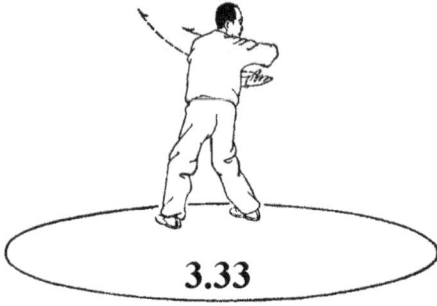

3.33

3.33

3.34 鸿雁出群   hóng yàn chū qún
Swan leaves the flock (left)

两足原地不动，上身左转；左掌从右肘下面向身体左上方移转上举，与头平齐；右掌同时臂外旋，随左掌转动，置于左肘里侧；两掌成仰掌，眼看左掌。

Turn the body to the left without moving the feet. Turn and lift the left palm from under the right elbow to head height at the upper left side of the body. Laterally rotate the right arm and follow the left palm with the right, placing it on the inside of the left elbow. Both palms are supine palms. Look at the left hand. (images 3.34a)

3.34a

3.34a

上动不停，左掌臂内旋，向身体左方转动，成竖掌；右掌随着臂内旋，屈肘向左肋侧下按，掌心向下；上身继续向左转动；头随着左掌向左方扭转，眼看左掌。

Medially rotate the left arm and bring it around to the left of the body, forming an upright palm. Medially rotate the right arm, bending the elbow to press the right hand down by the left side (palm facing down). Continue to turn the body to the left. Turn the head to the left as the left hand turns, following the hand with the eyes. (images 3.34b)

3.34b

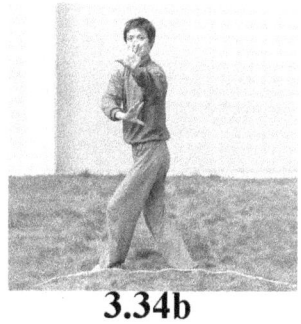

3.34b

第四掌

The Fourth Palm Change

左足尖外展，右足上步，开始从北向西，向南，向东，向北沿圆圈行走一周。走到北方原地点如图时，再换接下一式。

Hook out the left foot and step the right foot forward, then walk around the circle in a westerly direction, holding the same upper body posture as the images 3.34b. Start the next movement on returning to the North side.

要点：与第一掌第四动鸿雁出群同。

Pointers: Extend the left shoulder and elbow as far as possible around to the left, with the left palm at eyebrow height. Push and press the right palm down and forward, twist the waist to the left, and walk at an even pace.

4.1 紫燕抛翦 　　　　zǐ yàn pāo jiǎn

Violet Swallow Tosses Its Wings (right)

右足向左足前（西方）迈进一步，两足成倒八字步；左掌同时臂外旋，使拇指外侧向上，从右臂上面向右侧推出，掌心向外；右掌伸于左臂下面，小指外侧斜向上；两掌上下交迭；头向右转，眼看左掌。

Step the right foot in front of the left (West), forming the Chinese character eight 八. Laterally rotate the left arm (turn the thumb edge up) and push to the right over the right arm with the palm facing out. Extend the right palm along under the left arm with the little finger side on top. The arms are crossed, one above the other. Turn the head to the right, looking at the left hand. (images 4.1)

69

4.1

4.1

要点：与第一掌第五动紫燕抛翦同。

Pointers: Relax the shoulders, waist, and hips. Hold the arms in front of the chest in an embracing posture – do not cross them too tightly.

Translator's note: This is usually done in horse stance or a fairly large character eight stance. The previous step with the inside foot needs to turn out slightly to enable a larger step into the stance.

4.2   闭门推月   bì mén tuī yuè

   Close The Door And Push The Moon (left)

左足向身体左侧微移，足尖外展；上身稍向左转；左掌同时臂内旋使拇指外侧向下，从右向左屈肘带回，掌心向外；右掌同时臂外旋使掌指向下，向左下方推出，掌心斜向上；眼看两掌。

Shift the left foot to the left of the body, hooking the foot out. Turn the body slightly to the left. Medially rotate the left arm (so that the left thumb is on the bottom) and flex the elbow to draw the palm across to the left (palm facing out). Laterally rotate the right arm to point the fingers down, and push to the lower left with the palm facing up. Look at both hands. (images 4.2)

4.2

4.2

要点：与第一掌第六动闭门推月同。

Pointers: The arms form semi circles – they should not be too tightly bent.

4.3 金鸡撒膀 jīn jī sā bǎng

Golden Pheasant Shakes Its Wings (right)

左掌臂内旋使掌心向下，屈肘收于左腰侧，拇指在后，其余四指在前，成俯掌；右足同时向西南方伸出，右腿伸直；左足尖同时里扣，左腿屈膝下蹲；右掌随着顺着右腿反臂伸出，掌心反向上；头随着右掌向右扭转，上身前俯，眼看右掌。

Medially rotate the left arm (turn the palm down), flex the elbow and press the hand in a prone palm at waist height on the left side, with the thumb behind and the fingers in front. Step the right foot to the South-west and extend the leg. Squat on the left leg, turning the foot in. Extend the right palm out along the right leg with the arm rolled over, with the palm also rolled over to face up. Lean forward and turn the head to follow the movement of the right hand with the eyes. (images 4.3)

4.3

4.3

Translator's note: See my note with move 2.4.

4.4 移花接木 yí huā jiē mù

Move A Flower To Graft A Branch (right)

右足尖外展，上身直起，左腿伸直，左足随之进半步；右掌臂外旋使掌心向上，由下向上托起，成仰掌，肘微屈；眼看右掌。

Hook out the right foot and stand up, extending the left leg and stepping a half step in with the left foot. Laterally rotate the right arm (turn the palm up) and lift up with a supine palm with the elbow bent. Look at the right hand. (images 4.4)

要点：与第二掌第七动移花接木同，唯方向相反。

Pointers: Raise the head with the neck straight. Keep the power even in both legs. The right palm is at head height.

4.4

4.4

4.5   脑后摘盔   nǎo hòu zhāi kuī

Pick A Helmet Behind The Head (left)

左足向右足前方上步，足尖里扣，成倒八字步；身体同时右转；左
掌臂外旋使掌心向上，从左腰侧由右臂下面向右穿出；右掌位置不
变，两臂上下交迭；眼向右平视。

Hook in the left foot in front of the right, forming a Chinese character eight.
Turn the body to the right. Laterally rotate the left arm (turn the palm up)
and thread the hand out under the right arm to stab to the right. Keep the
right hand in the same position, so that the arms cross, one above the other.
Look to the right. (images 4.5a)

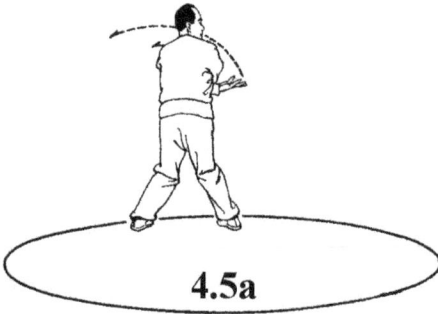

4.5a

4.5a

两足不动，左掌从右臂下面向左，向上斜摆上举，掌心仍向上；上
体随着左转；右掌顺势屈肘置于左肘里侧；眼看左掌。

Without moving the feet, swing the left palm under the right arm to the left
and up (palm still facing up). Turn the body to the left. Flex the right elbow
to keep the palm inside the left elbow. Look at the left hand. (images 4.5b)

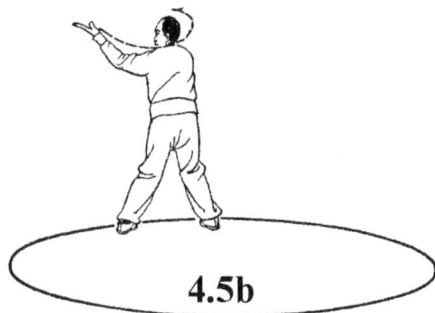

4.5b

4.5b

上动不停，左掌从左上方屈肘向脑后移转，至脑后时，向头顶上方托起；右掌从左肘里侧落至腹前，仍为仰掌；两眼平视。

Bend the left elbow and bring the palm down from the upper left to behind the head. Once it gets behind the head, push up above the head. Lower the right palm in front of the abdomen, keeping it in a supine palm. Look straight ahead. (images 4.5c)

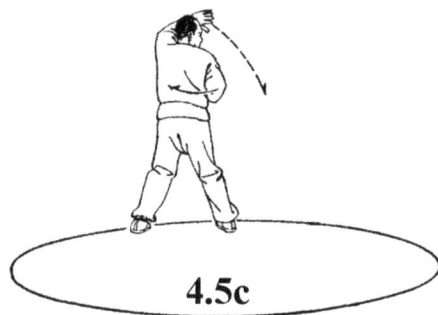

4.5c

4.5c

要点：与第二掌第八动脑后摘盔同，唯方向相反。

Pointers: Lift the head and relax the shoulders and hips. Keep the elbows bent.

4.6 蜀道横云 shǔ dào héng yún

The Sichuan Road Crosses The Clouds (left)

右足尖外展，左足向右足前方迈进一步，右腿后座；左掌同时由头顶上方屈肘向上身左前方下按，掌背向上，成横掌；右掌同时臂内旋掌心朝下，移于右腰侧；眼看左掌。

Hook out the right foot and step the left foot in front of the right, sitting back on the right leg. Bend the left arm and push down across the body to the front left (palm facing down). Medially rotate the right arm to place the palm down by the right waist. Look at the left hand. (images 4.6)

要点：左掌腕关节紧扣，与左足上下相对。

Pointers: Turn the left wrist in tightly, directly above the left foot.

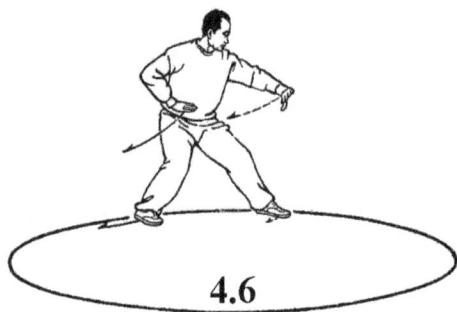

4.6

4.6

4.7   金鸡撒膀   jīn jī sā bǎng

Golden Pheasant Shakes Its Wings (right)

左掌屈肘收于左腰侧，拇指在后，其余四指在前，成俯掌；右足同时向西南方伸出，右腿伸直；左足尖同时里扣，左腿屈膝下蹲；右掌随着顺着右腿反臂伸出，掌心反向上；头随着右掌向右扭转，上身前俯，眼看右掌。

Bend the left elbow and sink the palm down by the left waist in a prone palm, with the thumb behind and the fingers in front. Step the right foot to the South-west and extend the leg. Squat on the left leg, turning the foot in. Extend the right palm out along the right leg with the arm rolled over, rolling the palm over to face up. Lean forward and turn the head right to watch the right hand. (images 4.7)

4.7

4.7

要点：与第二掌第六动金鸡撒膀同，唯方向相反。

Pointers: The weight is on the left leg, forming a right drop stance.

Translator's note: See my not with move 2.4.

4.8   移花接木   yí huā jiē mù

Move A Flower To Graft A Branch (right)

右足尖外展，上身直起，左腿伸直，左足随之进半步；右掌臂外旋使掌心向上，由下向上托起，成仰掌，肘微屈；眼看右掌。

Hook the right foot out and stand up, extending the left leg and stepping a half step in with the left foot. Laterally rotate the right arm to turn the palm up, flex the elbow and lift up with a supine palm. Look at the right hand. (images 4.8)

4.8

4.8

要点：与第二掌第七动移花接木同，唯方向相反。

Pointers: Raise the head with the neck straight and keep the strength evenly in both legs. The right palm is at head height.

4.9   乌龙缠腰   wū lóng chán yāo

Black Dragon Coils Its Body (left)

左足向右足前迈进一步，足尖里扣，两足成倒八字步；左掌同时臂外旋使掌心向上，从右臂下面向上屈肘托起，掌指向后；右掌同时屈肘收于左肘里侧，上身随之右转，眼看左掌。

Step the left foot in front of the right, hooking in to form the Chinese character eight 八. Laterally rotate the left arm to turn the palm up, and lift up from under the right arm with the fingers pointing back. Bend the right arm and bring the hand in to inside the left elbow. Turn right and look at the left hand. (images 4.9a)

4.9a

4.9a

上动不停，左掌从左侧由头后续向右侧，拇指外侧向下；上身随之
向右扭转，两足不动；右掌同时从身前经腹部屈肘绕向身后，掌指
贴身，拇指外侧向上；头右转，眼看右肘。

Coil the left hand around the back of the head from the left to the right side
with the thumb side on the bottom. Turn the body to the right without
moving the feet. Circle the right hand in front of the body, across the
abdomen to behind the body with the back of the hand touching the body
and the thumb side on top. Turn the head right and look at the right elbow.
(images 4.9b)

4.9b

4.9b

要点：在左掌上托时，左臂要屈成直角，左腕要屈紧，两腿弯曲，
两膝要向里紧扣，胸要内涵；在右掌缠腰时，两肩关节要放松使之
柔活，两掌和转身的动作要协调一致。

Pointers: When the left hand pushes up, bend the arm to form a right angle,
keeping the wrist tightly bent. Flex the knees, turning them in. Close in the
chest. When the right hand coils around the waist, the shoulders must be
relaxed and soft, so that the coiling actions of the hands and body are
coordinated.

4.10   走马活挟   zǒu mǎ huó xié

Scoop Up The Live Enemy On Horseback (right)

右足向东进半部，上身前移，右掌同时从背后向身前屈肘上举，掌心向里，掌指向上；左掌随之从上屈肘向胸前下按，拇指外侧向里；眼看右掌。

Step the right foot a half step to the East, moving the body forward. Lift the right hand up from behind the back to in front of the body with the elbow bent (palm facing in and fingers pointing up). Press the left hand down in front of the chest with the thumb side inside. Look at the right hand. (images 4.10)

4.10

4.10

要点：右掌稍高于头，左掌与右肘相对，两臂均屈成弧形；肩，胯要放松，两掌要用力。

Pointers: The right hand is slightly higher than the head. The left hand is opposite the right elbow. The arms roughly form a circle. Relax the shoulders and hips and put power into the palms.

Translator's note: Bring the right hand low around the low in the front before lifting to deflect. The left push is with the palm horizontal, thumb side down. Watch that this is different from Fierce Tiger Escapes from the Cage. Aside from the application being a bit different, there is a more rolling power set up for the following move.

4.11   行步撩衣   xíng bù liāo yī

Pull Up The Cloak While Walking Along (left)

右足尖里扣，上身左转，左足伸出半步，左腿伸直，右腿屈膝；右掌屈肘从身前下降，停于腹部右侧，掌心向下，成俯掌；左掌从身前向下，向左反臂上撩，掌心反向上；眼看左掌。

Hook in the right foot and turn the torso to the left, extending the left a half step. Extend the left leg and bend the right. Drop the right hand down in front of the body to the right side of the belly with the palm facing down in a prone palm. Swing the left hand down then left with the arm rolled over to roll the palm over to face up. Look at the left hand (images 4.11, and from behind)

4.11

4.11

4.11 from behind

4.11 from behind

要点：全身重量在右腿，上身前俯。

Pointers: Lean forward, put all the weight on the right leg.

Translator's note: This move has a number of variations. The lower hand can be extended as a rolled groin strike or throw. Note that Cai Yuhua is a bit more rolled into the back in the photo, and his weight is a bit more shifting between the legs. I also learned it this way.

4.12   推山入海   tuī shān rù hǎi

Push The Mountain Into The Sea (right)

左掌屈肘向下，向里，向上托起，掌心向上，掌指向前；左足尖外
展，上身左转；右足随之向左足前迈进一步，两腿屈膝略蹲；右掌
同时向身前平伸推出，掌指向上，肘微屈；眼看右掌。

Bend the left arm and bring the hand down, in, then lift up (the palm faces up and the fingers point forward). Hook out the left foot and turn the body left. Step the right foot in front of the left and flex both knees. Push the right hand straight out (fingers pointing up) with the elbow slightly bent. Look at the right hand. (images 4.12)

4.12

4.12

要点：动作要协调，两肩要放松，右掌掌指高与眉齐，左掌稍高过
头。推掌时右腕必屈紧。

Pointers: Keep the shoulders relaxed. The fingers of the right hand are at eyebrow height and the left hand is slightly higher than the head. Keep the right wrist tightly bent when pushing.

4.13   蝙蝠落地   biān fú luò dì

Bat Lands On The Ground (right)

右足向左足后方退一步，两腿屈膝成为歇步，左腿盖压在右腿上面，
右足跟离地掀起；右掌同时向上屈肘托起，腕关节略向外旋，拇指
对向面部，掌心向上；左掌随之落于右肘里侧，眼看右掌。

Step the right foot behind the left, bending both knees to form a resting stance, the left leg pressed on top of the right and the right heel off the ground. Push up with the right hand, laterally rotating the wrist so the thumb points to the face and the palm faces up. Keep the left hand inside the right elbow. Look at the right hand. (images 4.13a)

4.13a

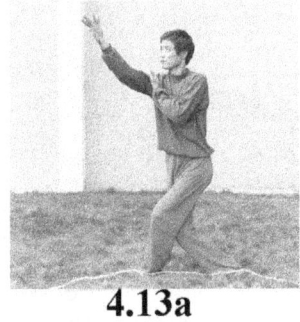

4.13a

右掌向外，向前，向里转腕平绕一圈，随既反臂向前平伸撩出，掌心反向上；两腿随之向下沉坐，左掌同时向身后反臂伸出，掌心反向上；眼看右掌。

Turn the right wrist on a horizontal plane, circling the hand out, forward, then in, then turn the arm over and swing up to extend horizontally to the front with the palm turned over to face up. Sit further down on the legs, extending the left hand out to the back with the arm rolled over to roll the palm over to face up. Look at the right hand. (images 4.13b)

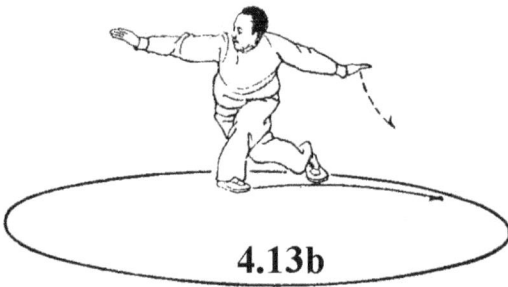

4.13b

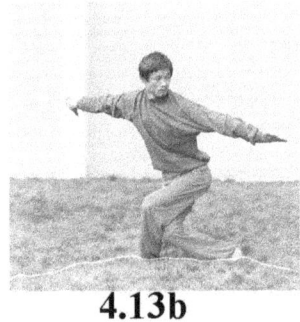

4.13b

要点：歇步时，左足尖必须外展，两腿迭紧，右掌高与头齐；右掌平绕时，必须以腕关节为轴转动，反撩之后，掌高稍国右肩。

Pointers: The resting stance is done with the left foot turned out and the legs held tightly together. The right hand is at head height. When circling the right hand, make sure to pivot around the wrist. After rolling the arm over, the palm strikes slightly higher than the shoulder.

Translator's note: See in the photo 4.13a, Cai Yuhua is in mid rotatation of his wrist. The right hand does a flat cut as you step back, then rolls to stab as you sit down. See images 4.13b, you should be looking at the high hand, the right, when sitting down. In the photo, Cai has already shifted his gaze to the other side.

4.14   飞燕抄水   fēi yàn chāo shuǐ

Flying Swallow Skims The Water (left)

左足向东仆腿伸出，足尖里扣；右足跟落地踏实，成为仆步；左掌
顺势直臂下沉， 头向左转，眼看左掌。

Extend the left foot to the East, with the foot turned in. Settle onto the right
heel to form a drop stance. Straighten the left arm and settle it down. Turn
the head left to look at the left hand. (images 4.14)

4.14

4.14

要点：全身重量，坐于右腿。

Pointers: Sit all the weight onto the right leg.

4.15   怀中抱月   huái zhōng bào yuè

Embrace The Moon In The Bosom (left)

上身直起，左足尖稍外展，右足随着前移半步，两腿微屈；右掌同
时屈肘收于右腰侧，掌指向前，掌心向下；左掌随着臂外旋使拇指
外侧向上，掌心向里，屈肘环抱，作抱腰式；眼看左掌。

Stand up, hook out the left foot and move the right foot a half step forward,
bending both knees. Bring the right hand in by the right side with the
fingers pointing forward and the palm facing down. Laterally rotate the left
arm and form an embracing position with the thumb on top and the palm
facing in. Look at the left hand. (images 4.15)

4.15

4.15

要点：与第二掌第九动怀中抱月同。

Pointers: Bend the legs with the strength evenly distributed. Bend the left arm in a semi circle with the left palm at chest height.

4.16   叶底藏花   yè dǐ cáng huā

Hide A Flower Under A Leaf (left)

右足向左足前方迈进一步，足尖里扣；两腿微屈；上身左转朝向北方；左掌同时臂内旋使拇指外侧朝下，屈肘向左带平；右掌随之臂外旋使掌心向上，向左腋下穿出。

Hook in the right foot in front of the left. Keep the legs bent. Turn the body to the left, towards the North. Medially rotate the left arm (turn the thumb side down), flex the left elbow and draw the palm across to the left. Laterally rotate the right arm to turn the palm up, and stab under the left armpit. (images 4.16)

4.16

4.16

要点：与第一掌第三动叶底藏花同，唯方向相反。

Pointers: Turn the head to the left to look at the left elbow.

4.17 鸿雁出群   hóng yàn chū qún

Swan Leaves The Flock (right)

两足原地不动，上身右转；右掌从左肘下面向身体右上方移转上举
与头平齐；左掌同时臂外旋，随右掌转动，置于右肘里侧；两掌成
仰掌，眼看右掌。

Turn the body to the right without moving the feet. Rotate and lift the right
palm from below the left elbow to head height at the upper right of the body
(South-east). Laterally rotate the left arm and follow the movement of the
right hand, keeping the hand inside the right elbow. Both palms are supine
palms. Look at the right hand. (images 4.17a)

4.17a

4.17a

上动不停，右掌臂内旋，向身体右方转动，成竖掌；左掌随着臂内
旋，屈肘向右侧下按，掌心向下；上身继续向右转动；头随着右掌
向右方扭转，眼看右掌。

Medially rotate the right arm and turn the hand to the right of the body in
an upright palm. Medially rotate the left arm and flex the elbow to press the
hand down by the right side with the palm facing down. Continue to turn
the body to the right. Turn the head to follow the movement of the right
hand. (images 4.17b)

4.17b

4.17b

右足尖外展，左足上步，开始从北向东，向南，向西，向北沿圆圈
行走一周。走到北方原起点如图时，再换接下一式。

Hook out the right foot and step the left forward, starting to walk eastward around the circle holding the same posture as figure 4.17b. Start the next move after completing a full circle and returning to the North side.

要点：与第一掌四动鸿雁出群同，唯方向相反。

Pointers: Extend the right shoulder and elbow as far as possible around to the right, with the right palm at eyebrow height. Push and press the left palm down and forward. Twist the waist to the right and walk at an even pace.

4.18　紫燕抛翦　　　　　zě yàn pāo jiǎn

　　Violet Swallow Tosses Its Wings (left)

左足向右足前（东方）迈进一步，两足成倒八字步；右掌同时臂外
旋，使拇指外侧向上，从左臂上面向左侧推出，掌心向外；左掌伸
于右臂下面，小指外侧斜向上；两掌上下交迭，头向左转，眼看右
掌。

Hook in the left foot in front of the right (East), forming the Chinese character eight 八. Laterally rotate the right arm (turn the thumb side on top) and push to the left over the left arm with the palm facing out. Extend the left palm out under the right arm with the little finger side on top. The arms are crossed, one above the other. Turn the head to the left, looking at the right hand. (images 4.18)

4.18

4.18

4.19 闭门推月   bì mén tuī yuè

Close The Door And Push The Moon (right)

右足向身体右侧微移，足尖外展；上身稍向右转；右掌同时臂内旋
使拇指外侧向下，从左向右屈肘带回，掌心向外；左掌同时臂外旋
使掌指向下，向右下方推出，掌心斜向上；眼看两掌。

Shift the right foot slightly to the right of the body, hooking out. Turn the
torso slightly to the right. Medially rotate the right arm turning the thumb
edge to the bottom and flex the elbow to draw the palm to the right with the
palm facing out. Laterally rotate the left arm so that the fingers point down
and push to the lower right (palm facing diagonally up). Look at both hands.
(images 4.19)

4.19

4.19

4.20 金鸡撒膀   jīn jī sā bǎng

Golden Pheasant Shakes Its Wings (left)

右掌臂内旋使掌心向下，屈肘收于右腰侧，拇指在后，其余四指在
前，成俯掌；左足同时向东南方伸出，左腿伸直；右足尖同时里扣，
右腿屈膝下蹲；左掌随之顺着左腿反臂伸出，掌心反向上；头随着
左掌向左扭转，上身前俯，眼看左掌。

Medially rotate the right arm to turn the palm down, flex the elbow and
bring the hand in by the right side forming a prone palm at the waist
(thumb behind and fingers in front). Extend the left foot to the South-east
and extend the leg. Squat on the right leg, turning the foot in. Roll the left
arm over and slide the left hand out along the left leg, with the palm rolled
over to face up. Turn the head left to watch the left palm and lean forward.
(images 4.20)

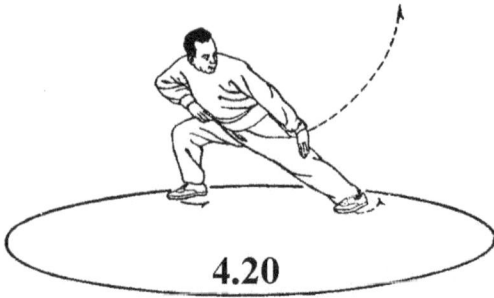

4.20

4.20

4.21　移花接木　　　　yí huā jiē mù

Move A Flower To Graft A Branch (left)

左足尖外展，上身直起，右腿伸直，右足随之进半步；左掌臂外旋使掌心向上，由下向上托起，成仰掌，肘微屈；眼看左掌。

Hook the left foot out and stand up, extending the right leg and stepping in a half step with the right foot. Laterally rotate the left arm (turn the palm up) and lift up in a supine palm with the elbow bent. Look at the left hand. (images 4.21)

4.21

4.21

4.22　脑后摘盔　　　　nǎo hòu zhāi kuī

Pick A Helmet Behind The Head (right)

右足向左足前方上步，足尖里扣，成倒八字步；身体同时左转；右掌臂外旋使掌心向上，从右腰侧由左臂下面向左穿出；左掌位置不变，两臂上下交迭；眼看右掌。

Step with the right foot hooking in, in front of the left, forming a Chinese character eight 八. Turn the body to the left. Laterally rotate the right arm to turn the palm up, and thread it out under the left arm to stab to the left. Keep the left hand in the same position, so that the arms cross, one above the other. (images 4.22a)

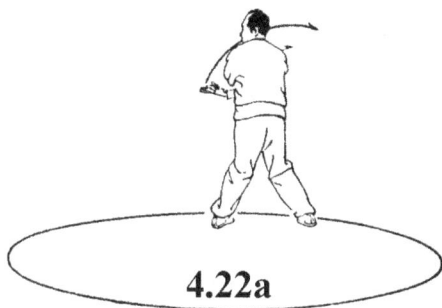

4.22a

4.22a

两足不动，右掌从左臂下面向右，向上斜摆上举，掌心仍向上；上体随着右转；左掌顺势屈肘置于右肘里侧；眼看右掌。

Without moving the feet, swing the right palm up from under the right arm to the right and lift up (palm still facing up). Turn the body to the right. Flex the left elbow to keep the palm inside the right elbow. Look at the right hand. (images 4.22b)

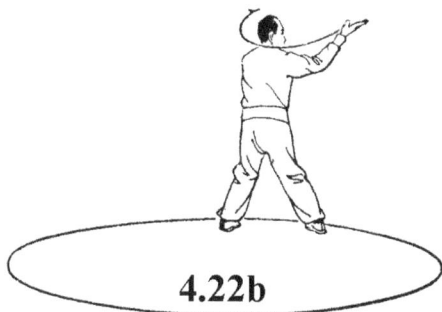

4.22b

4.22b

上动不停，右掌从右上方屈肘向脑后移转，至脑后时，向头顶上方托起；左掌从右肘里侧落至腹前，仍为仰掌；两眼平视。

Bend the right elbow and bring the palm down behind the head from the upper right. Once it gets behind the head, push up above the head. Lower the left palm inside the right elbow to in front of the abdomen, keeping it in a supine palm. Look straight ahead. (images 4.22c)

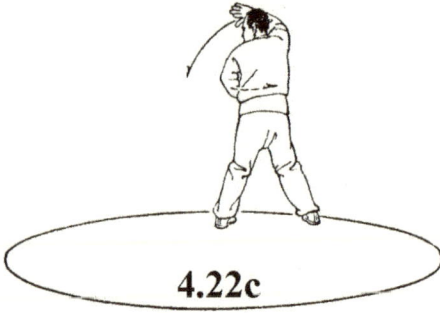

4.22c

4.22c

4.23   蜀道横云   shǔ dào héng yún

The Sichuan Road Crosses The Clouds (right)

左足尖外展，右足向作足前方迈进一步，作腿后座；右掌同时由头顶上方屈肘向上身右前方下按，掌背向上，成横掌；作掌同时臂内旋掌心朝下，移于作腰侧；眼看右掌。

Hook the left foot out and step the right foot in front of the left, sitting back on the left leg. Bend the right arm to press down from above the head to the forward right with the palm facing down across the body. Medially rotate the left arm to place the palm down by the right waist, look at the right hand. (images 4.23)

4.23

4.23

4.24   金鸡撒膀   jīn jī sā bǎng

Golden Pheasant Shakes Its Wings (left)

右掌屈肘收于右腰侧，拇指在后，其余四指在前，成俯掌；左足同时向东南方伸出，左腿伸直；右足尖同时里扣，右腿屈膝下蹲；左掌随之顺着左腿反臂伸出，掌心反向上；头随着左掌向左，上身前俯，眼看左掌。

Bend the right elbow and sink the palm down by the right waist in a prone palm (thumb behind and fingers in front). Extend the left foot to the Southeast and extend the leg. Squat on the right leg, turning the foot in. Slide the left palm out along the left leg with the arm rolled over, with the palm also rolled over to face up. Turn the head to follow the left hand and lean forward, looking at the left hand. (images 4.24)

4.24

4.24

4.25 移花接木　　　yí huā jiē mù

Move A Flower To Graft A Branch (left)

左足尖外展，上身直起，右腿伸直，右足随之进半步；左掌臂外旋使掌心向上，由下向上托起，成仰掌，肘微屈；眼看左掌。

Hook out the left foot and stand up, extending the right leg and stepping in a half step with the right foot. Laterally rotate the left arm (turn the palm up) and lift up with a supine palm with the elbow bent. Look at the left hand. (images 4.25)

4.25

4.25

4.26 乌龙缠腰　　　wū lóng chán yāo

Black Dragon Coils Its Body (right)

右足向左足前迈进一步，足尖里扣，两足成倒八字步；右掌同时臂外旋使掌心向上，从左臂下面向上屈肘托起，掌指向后；左掌同时屈肘收于右肘里侧，上身随之左转，眼看右掌。

Step the right foot in front of the left, hooking in, forming the Chinese character eight. Laterally rotate the right arm (turn the palm up) and lift up from under the left arm with the fingers pointing back. Bend the left arm and bring the hand inside the right elbow. Turn left and look at the right hand. (images 4.26a)

4.26a

4.26a

上动不停，右掌从右侧由头后续向左侧，拇指外侧向下；上身随之向左扭转，两足不动；左掌同时从身前经腹部屈肘绕向身后，掌指贴身，拇指外侧向上；头左转，眼看左肘。

Coil the right hand around the back of the head from the right to the left side with the thumb side on the bottom. Twist the body to the left without moving the feet. Circle the left hand across in front of the abdomen to behind the body with the back of the hand touching the body and the thumb side on top. Turn the head left and look at the left elbow. (images 4.26b)

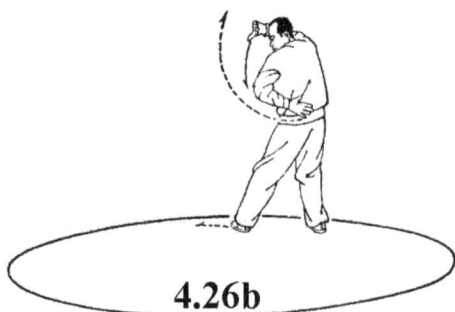

4.26b

4.26b

4.27   走马活挟   zǒu mǎ huó xié
Scoop Up The Live Enemy On Horseback (left)

左足向西进半部，上身前移，左掌同时从背后向身前屈肘上举，掌心向里，掌指向上；右掌随之从上屈肘向胸前下按，拇指外侧向里；眼看左掌。

Step the left foot a half step to the West, moving the body forward. Lift the left hand up behind the back to in front of the body with the elbow bent (palm facing in and fingers pointing up). Press the right hand down in front of the chest with the thumb side inside. Look at the left hand. (images 4.27)

4.27

4.27

4.28   行步撩衣   xíng bù liāo yī

Pull Up The Cloak While Walking Along (right)

左足尖里扣，上身右转，右足伸出半步，右腿伸直，左腿屈膝；左掌屈肘从身前下降，停于腹部左侧，掌心向下，成俯掌；右掌从身前向下，向右反臂上撩，掌心反向上；眼看右掌。

Turn the left foot in while turning the body to the right, extending the right foot a half step. Extend the right leg and bend the left. Press the left hand down in front of the body to the left side of the abdomen with the palm facing down in a prone palm. Bring the right hand down, then right, then swing up with the arm rolled over and the palm rolled over to face up. Look at the right hand. (images 4.28)

4.28

4.28

4.29　推山入海　　　　tuī shān rù hǎi

Push The Mountain Into The Sea (left)

右掌屈肘向下，向里，向上托起，掌心向上，掌指向前；右足尖外
展，上身右转；左足随之向右足前迈进一步，两腿屈膝略蹲；左掌
同时向身前平伸推出，掌指向上，肘微屈；眼看左掌。

Bend the right arm and bring the hand down and in, then lift up with the
palm facing up and the fingers pointing forward. Turn the right foot out and
turn the body right. Then step the left foot in front of the right and flex both
knees. Push straight forward with the left hand (fingers pointing up) with
the elbow slightly bent. Look at the left hand. (images 4.29)

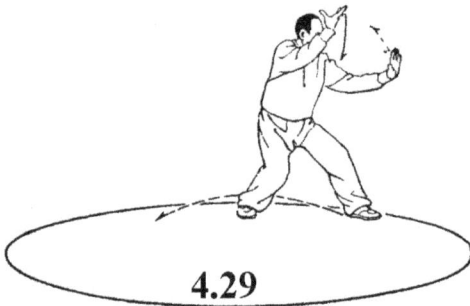

4.29

4.29

4.30　蝙蝠落地　　　　biān fú luò dì

Bat Lands On The Ground (left)

左足向右足后方退一步，两腿屈膝成为歇步，右腿盖压在左腿上面，
左足跟离地掀起；左掌同时向上屈肘托起，腕关节略向外旋，拇指
对向面部，掌心向上；右掌随之落于左肘里侧，眼看左掌。

Step the left foot back behind the right, bending both knees to form a
resting stance – the right leg pressed on top of the left and the left heel off
the ground. Push up with the left hand, laterally rotating the wrist so the
thumb points to the face and the palm faces up. Lower the right hand inside
the left elbow. Look at the left hand. (images 4.30a)

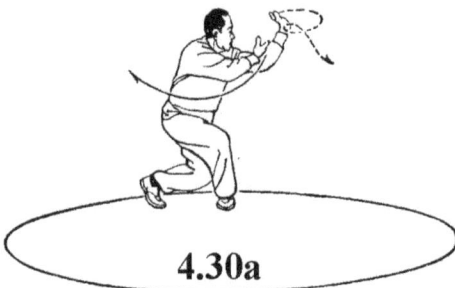

4.30a

4.30a

左掌向外，向前，向里转腕平绕一圈，随既反臂向前平伸撩出，掌心反向上；两腿随之向下沉坐，右掌同时向身后反臂伸出，掌心反向上；眼看左掌。

Circle the left hand on a horizontal plane around its wrist, out, forward, then in, then turn the arm over and swing it up, extending it to the front with the palm rolled over to face up. Sit further down on the legs, extending the right hand out to the back with the arm rolled over so that the palm is turned over to face up. Look at the left hand. (images 4.30b)

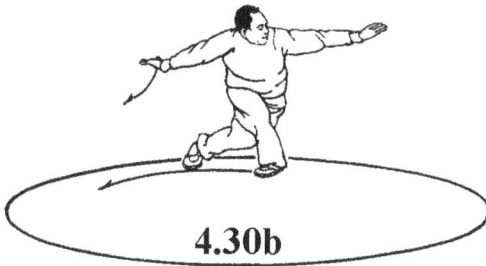

4.30b

4.30b

4.31   飞燕抄水   fēi yàn chāo shuǐ

Flying Swallow Skims The Water (right)

右足向西仆腿伸出，足尖里扣；左足跟落地踏实，成为仆步；右掌顺势直臂下沉， 头向右转，眼看右掌。

Extend the right foot to the West, with the foot turned in. Settle onto the left heel in a drop stance. Straighten the right arm and settle it down. Turn the head right and look at the right hand. (images 4.31)

4.31

4.31

4.32 怀中抱月   huái zhōng bào yuè

Embrace The Moon In The Bosom (right)

上体直起，右足尖稍外展，左足随着前移半部，两腿稍屈；左掌同
时屈肘收于左腰前，拇指向后，掌心向下； 右掌随之臂外旋使拇
指外侧向上，掌心向里，屈肘环抱，作抱腰式；眼看右掌。

Stand up, hook out the right foot and move the left foot a half step forward,
bending both legs. Bring the left hand in to by the left waist with the fingers
to the front and the palm facing down. Laterally rotate the right arm and
form an embracing position with the thumb on top and the palm facing in.
Look at the right hand. (images 4.32)

4.32

4.32

4.33 猿猴偷桃   yuán hóu tōu táo

Monkey Steals A Peach (right)

左足向右足前迈进一步，足尖里扣，两腿屈膝；上身随之右转朝向
北方；左掌同时从右肘下面向右穿出，掌心向下；右掌则臂内旋使
掌心向下，在身体转时屈肘环抱胸前；眼看右肘。

Hook in the left foot in front of the right, with the knees bent. Turn the torso
to the right towards the North. Thread the left hand under the right elbow
to stab to the right (palm facing down). Medially rotate the right arm to turn
the palm down and flex the elbow as the body turns, to embrace in front of
the chest. Look at the right elbow. (images 4.33, and from behind)

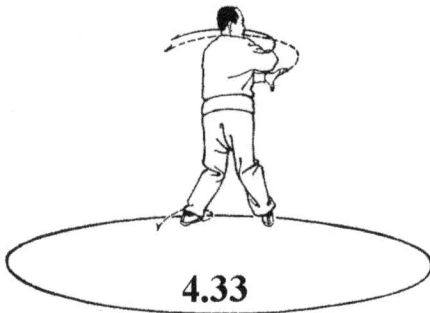

4.33

4.33

4.33 from behind

4.33 from behind

要点：头向右转， 两腿弯曲，两肩放松。

Pointers: Turn the head right. Keep the legs bent. Relax the shoulders.

Translator's note: Remember in Monkey Steals a Peach to Monkey Offers Fruit, to turn both palms down, then roll both together to turn up.

4.34   猿猴献果   yuán hóu xiàn guǒ

Monkey Offers Fruit (left)

左足尖外展，右脚尖里扣，上身随着左转，左掌同时臂外旋使掌心向上，从右向前屈肘平摆，至胸前时，掌指向左；右掌随之臂内旋使掌心反向上，从左向里，向右转动，掌指向右，在胸前胸前和左掌相并作捧物状；眼看两掌。

Hook the left foot out and the right foot in, turning the torso to the left. Medially rotate the left arm to turn the palm up, and swing it horizontally from the right to the front, bending the elbow– when it arrives in front of the chest, the fingers point left. Medially rotate the right arm to roll the palm over to face up, and turn it from the left to the inside then right with the fingers pointing right in front of the chest. The hands form a position as if to cup an object in both hands. Look at both hands. (images 4.34)

4.34

4.34

要点：两掌屈肘高于肩平，两肘下垂，两肩放松。

Pointers: Bend the elbows to place the hands at shoulder height with the elbows dropped and the shoulders relaxed.

4.35 大鹏展翅   dà péng zhǎn chì

Great Roc Spreads Its Wings (left)

两足原地不动，两掌向上体两侧平伸，掌心仍向上；眼看左掌。

Without moving the feet, extend both hands out horizontally to the side with the palms still facing up. Look at the left hand. (images 4.35)

4.35

4.35

第五掌

The Fifth Palm Change

左足尖外展，右足上步，开始从北向西，向南，向东，向北沿圆圈行走一周。走到北方原地起点如图时，再换接下一式。

Hook out the left foot and step the right foot forward, starting to walk around the circle in a westerly direction, holding the upper body posture as in images 4.35. Start the next movement after walking a complete circle back to the original place on the North side.

5.1　　十字搬搂　　　　shí zì bān lōu

Block With A Cross (right)

右足向左足前迈进一步，两足成倒八字步；右掌屈肘从右向左平伸，左掌同时屈肘从左向右由右臂上面平伸穿出，两掌心都向上，两臂作十字交叉状；眼看左掌。

Step the right foot in front of the left, forming the Chinese character eight 八. Flex the right elbow and extend the hand horizontally to the left. Bend the left elbow and extend the hand to the right, threading over the right arm (both palms up). The arms cross to form a Chinese character ten 十. Look at the left hand. (images 5.1)

5.1

要点：松肩沉肘，两掌稍低于胸部，两腿屈膝略蹲。

Pointers: Relax the shoulders and sink the elbows. The hands are slightly below chest height. The knees are slightly bent.

Translator's note: The text says to threaad the left hand over the right arm, but the action is more like a crossing sweep with both arms, meeting in the middle, left over right.

5.2 顺势领衣　　shùn shì lǐng yī

Take The Opportunity To Pull The Cloak (left

上身左转，左足前迈进半部，右足跟进半步，两腿屈膝；左掌同时从右向前，向左屈肘平摆；右掌随着移左肘里侧下方；两掌心都向上；眼看两掌。

Turn the torso left and step the left foot a half step forward, then bring the right foot up a half step towards it, with the knees bent. Swing the left hand flat across from the right to the front then towards the left. Move the right hand to inside and under the left elbow. The palms face up. Look at both hands. (images 5.2)

5.2

5.2

要点：头往上顶，松肩沉肘，两掌高于胸齐。

Pointers: Lift the head. Relax the shoulders and sink the elbows – the hands are at chest height.

Translator's note: The left foot and arm end up aligned on the circle line. The right hand is already under the left arm, so mostly goes along with the sweeping action.

5.3 横扫千军　　héng sǎo qiān jūn

Sweep Aside An Army Of A Thousand (right)

右足向左足前上一步，足尖外展，右掌同时向上体右后方屈肘平摆，左掌则屈肘移于右肘下端，两掌心仍向上；眼看右掌。

Step the right foot forward, hooking out in front of the left. Swing the right arm flat across to the right and rear of the torso with the elbow bent. Move the left hand under the right elbow with the elbow bent. The palms face up as before. Look at the right hand. (images 5.3)

5.3

5.3

要点：腰向右拧转，两臂屈肘，右掌高于肩齐。

Pointers: Twist the waist to the right. Keep the elbows bent. The right hand is at shoulder height.

Translator's note: The hook is a curl in then step out with a trample to the edge, on the circle line. The right arm ends up pointing into the centre of the circle.

5.4   横扫千军   héng sǎo qiān jūn

Sweep Aside An Army Of A Thousand (left)

上身左转向西，右足尖里扣，左足尖外展，两膝稍屈；左掌同时从右向身前，向左后平摆，肘微屈，右掌随着从右向身前，向左胸屈肘平摆，两掌心都向上；眼看左掌。

Turn the torso to the left to face West, hook the right foot in and the left foot out, with the knees bent. Swing the left arm flat across from the right to the front, then to the rear left of the body, with the elbow bent. Swing the right arm from the right then forward to the left of the chest. Both palms face up. Look at the left hand. (images 5.4)

5.4

5.4

要点：腰向左拧转，松肩沉肘，左掌稍低于肩部。

Pointers: Twist the waist to the left. Relax the shoulders and sink the elbows
– the left hand is slightly below shoulder height.

5.5   鹞子反身   yào zi fǎn shēn

Sparrow Hawk Rolls Over (right)

上身以左脚掌为轴左转向东；右脚在转身时离地提起，在转身后落
于左脚前，脚尖里扣；两腿膝稍屈；右掌在上身左转时，从左肘下
面向左穿出，左掌随着屈肘移于右侧，两掌心都向上；眼看左掌。

Turn the body around to the left to face East, pivoting on the ball of the left
foot. Lift the right foot as the body turns and place the foot hooked in in
front of the left foot as the turn is completed. Flex the knees. As the body
turns, thread the right hand under the left elbow out to the left, and flex the
left elbow to bring the left hand in to the right side. Both palms face up.
Look at the left hand. (images 5.5a)

5.5a

5.5a

上身左转向北；右掌同时臂内旋，从身前屈肘上举，拇指外侧向下，
掌心向前；左掌落至腹部，仍为仰掌；眼向左平看。

Turn the body to the left to face North. Medially rotate the right arm and lift
the hand up in front of the body with the thumb side down and the palm
facing forward. Lower the left hand to the abdomen, keeping a supine palm.
Look levelly to the left. (images 5.5b)

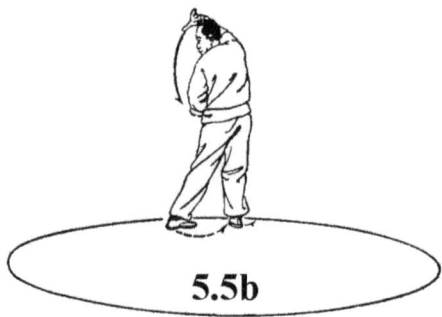

5.5b

5.5b

要点：两动必须连贯起来做，不要间断；至后一动时，腰向左拧，两肩松沉。

Pointers: The movement must be continuous. To connect with the following movement, twist the waist left and keep the shoulders relaxed and settled.

Translator's note: In the images 5.5a, Cai Yuhua has extended further than Jiang. He is just further along in the move.

5.6   金鸡筝斗   jīn jī zhēng dòu
Golden Pheasant Fights (left)

右脚跟外展，上身左转向西；左足退于右足内侧，以足尖点地；两腿屈膝略蹲；右掌同时由左肩下降经腹部，落至右腰侧，拇指外侧向上，掌心向前；左掌随之由腹部落至左腰侧，拇指外侧向上，掌心向前；眼向前平看。

Hook out the right foot and turn the body to the left to face West. Bring the left foot in to inside the right, touching the toes to the ground. Flex the knees, lower the right hand down past the left shoulder and across the belly to by the right side of the waist. Bring the left hand across the belly to by the left side of the waist – both hands have the thumb edge on top and the palm facing forward. Look straight ahead. (images 5.6a)

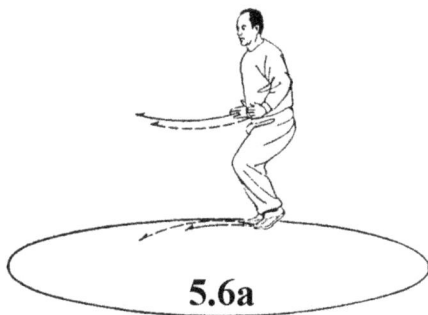

5.6a

5.6a

左足向前进一步，右足跟进半步，两腿屈膝，上身后坐；两掌同时向前屈肘推出，掌腕相并，拇指外侧都向上；眼看两掌。

Step the left foot forward then bring the right foot a half step towards it, sitting back with the knees bent. Push forward with both hands, with the elbows bent and the wrists together, the thumbs on top. Look at both hands. (images 5.6b)

要点：第一动两腿略蹲时，身体重量落于右腿，两肩要松沉；第二动推掌后，要沉肩垂肘，两小臂与地面成水平。

Pointers: In the first part of the movement, sit on the right leg, keep the shoulders relaxed and settled. In the second part, after pushing, settle the shoulders and sink the elbows – keep the forearms parallel with the ground.

5.6b

5.6b

5.7   怀中抱月   huái zhōng bào yuè

Embrace The Moon In The Bosom (left)

左足向身后退回一大步，上身随着左转，右足尖里扣，两腿屈膝；
左掌同时臂内旋使拇指外侧向上，屈肘作抱腰式；右掌则屈肘收于
右腰侧，拇指向后，其余四指在前，掌心向下；眼看左掌。

Take a large step backwards with the left foot, turning the body to the left, turning the right foot in, and bending the knees. Medially rotate the left arm and lower the hand in front of the body, turning the hand over then lifting it up to the front. Once the hand is raised horizontally, laterally rotate the arm (turn the thumb side up) and flex the elbow in an embracing posture. Bring the right hand in to the right side of the waist with the palm facing down, the thumb behind and the fingers in front. Look at the left hand. (images 5.7)

5.7

5.7

要点：与第二掌第九动怀中抱月同。

Pointers: Flex the legs with the power evenly distributed. Flex the left arm in a semi circle with the left palm at chest height.

5.8 猿猴偷桃 yuán hóu tōu táo
Monkey Steals A Peach (left)

右足向左足前迈进一步，足尖里扣，两腿屈膝；上身随之左转朝向北方；右掌同时从左肘下面向左穿出，掌心向下；左掌则臂内旋使掌心向下，在上身体左转时屈肘环抱胸前；眼看左肘。

Hook in the right foot in front of the left with the knees bent. Turn the body to the left towards the North. Thread the right hand under the left elbow to stab to the left with the palm facing down. Then medially rotate the left arm (turn the palm down) and flex the elbow as the body turns left, to embrace in front of the chest. Look at the left elbow. (images 5.8, and photo 5.8 from behind.)

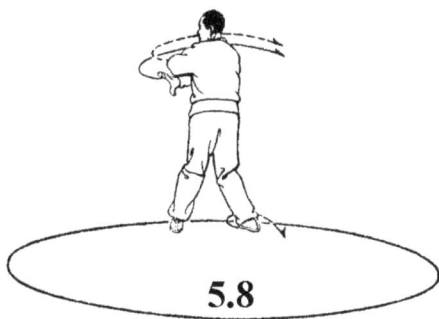

5.8

5.8

5.8 from behind

5.9 猿猴献果 yuán hóu xiàn guǒ
Monkey Offers Fruit (right)

右足尖外展，左脚尖里扣，上身随着右转，右掌同时臂外旋使掌心向上，从左向前屈肘平摆，至胸前时，掌指向右；左掌随之臂内旋使掌心反向上，从右向里，向左转动，掌指向左，在胸前胸前和右掌相并作捧物状；眼看两掌。

Hook the right foot out and the left foot in, turning the body to the right. Medially rotate the right arm (turn the palm up) and swing it horizontally forward from the left with the elbow bent – as it arrives in front of the chest the fingers point right. Medially rotate the left arm (turn the palm over and up) then turn it from the right to the inside then left with the fingers pointing left. The hands form a position like cupping an object in the hands in front of the chest. Look at both hands .(images 5.9)

5.9

5.9

5.10 大鵬展翅   dà péng zhǎn chì
Great Roc Spreads Its Wings (right)

两足原地不动，两掌向上体两侧平伸，掌心仍向上；眼看右掌。

Without moving the feet, extend both hands out horizontally to the side with the palms still facing up. Look at the right hand. (images 5.10)

5.10

5.10

左足尖外展，右足上步，开始从北向西，向南，向东，向北沿圆圈行走一周。走到北方原地起点如图时，再换接下一式。

Hook out the right foot and step the left foot forward, starting to walk around the circle in an easterly direction holding the upper body posture of figure 5.10. Walk a complete circle until you arrive in the original place on the North side, then continue to the next movement.

5.11 十字搬搂   shí zì bān lōu

Block With A Cross (left)

左足向右足前迈进一步，两足成倒八字步；左掌屈肘从左向右平伸，右掌同时屈肘从右向左由左臂上面平伸穿出，两掌心都向上，两臂作十字交叉状；眼看右掌。

Hook in the left foot in front of the right, forming the Chinese character eight 八. Flex the left elbow and extend the hand horizontally to the right, while bending the right elbow and threading the hand over the left arm to stab to the left. Both palms face up. The arms cross to form the Chinese character ten 十. Look at the right hand. (images 5.11)

5.11

5.11

5.12 顺势领衣   shùn shì lǐng yī

Take The Opportunity To Pull The Cloak (left)

上身右转，右足前迈进半部，左足跟进半步，两腿屈膝；右掌同时从左向前，向右屈肘平摆；左掌随着移右肘里侧下方；两掌心都向上；眼看两掌。

Turn the body right and step the right foot a half step forward, then bring the left foot up a half step, with the knees bent. Swing the right hand horizontally forward from the left then to the right. Move the left hand to inside and under the right elbow. The palms face up. Look at the right hand.

5.12

5.12

(images 5.12)

5.13　横扫千军　　　　héng sǎo qiān jūn

Sweep Aside An Army Of A Thousand (left)

左足向右足前上一步，足尖外展，左掌同时向上体右后方屈肘平摆，右掌则屈肘移于左肘下端，两掌心仍向上；眼看左掌。

Hook out the left foot in front of the right. Swing the left arm horizontally to the left and rear of the body with the elbow bent. Slide the right hand to below the left elbow with the elbow bent. Both palms face up as before. Look at the left hand. (images 5.13)

5.13

5.13

5.14　横扫千军　　　　héng sǎo qiān jūn

Sweep Aside An Army Of A Thousand (right)

上身右转向东，左足尖里扣，右足尖外展，两膝稍屈；右掌同时从左向身前，向右后平摆，肘微屈，左掌随着从左向身前，向右胸屈肘平摆，两掌心都向上；眼看右掌。

Turn the body to the right to face East, hook the left foot in and the right foot out, with the knees bent. Swing the right arm horizontally forward from the left, then to the right rear of the body, with the elbow bent. Swing the left arm forward to the right chest. The palms face up. Look at the right hand. (images 5.14)

5.14

5.14

5.15 鹞子反身   yào zǐ fǎn shēn

Sparrow Hawk Rolls Over (left)

上身以右脚掌为轴右转向西；左脚在转身时离地提起，在转身后落于右脚前，脚尖里扣；两腿膝稍屈；左掌在上身右转时，从右肘下面向右穿出，右掌随着屈肘移于左侧，两掌心都向上；眼看右掌。

Turn the body around to the right to face West, pivoting on the ball of the right foot. Lift the left foot as the body turns, and place it hooked in, in front of the right foot as the turn is completed. Flex the knees. As the body turns thread the left hand under the right elbow to stab out to the right, and flex the right elbow to bring the right hand in to the left side. Both palms face up. Look at the right hand. (images 5.15a)

5.15a

5.15a

上身右转向北；左掌同时臂内旋，从身前屈肘上举，拇指外侧向下，掌心向前；右掌落至腹部，仍为仰掌；眼向右平看。

Turn the body to the right to face North. Medially rotate the left arm and lift the hand up in front of the body with the thumb side down and the palm facing forward. Lower the right hand to the abdomen, keeping a supine palm. Look levelly to the right. (images 5.15b)

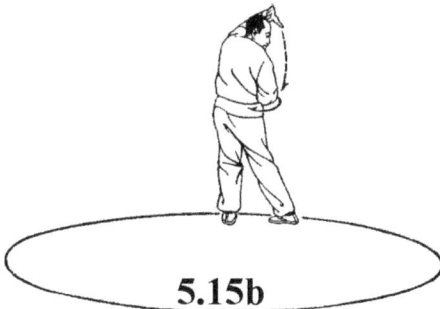

5.15b

5.15b

5.16   金鸡筝斗   jīn jī zhēng dòu

Golden Pheasant Fights (right)

左脚跟外展，上身右转向东；右足退于左足内侧，以足尖点地；两
腿屈膝略蹲；左掌同时由右肩下降经腹部，落至左腰侧，拇指外侧
向上，掌心向前；右掌随之由腹部落至右腰侧，拇指外侧向上，掌
心向前；眼向前平看。

Hook out the left foot and turn the body to the right to face East. Bring the
right foot in to inside the left, touching the toes to the ground. Flex the
knees. Lower the left hand down past the right shoulder and across the
abdomen to the left side of the waist. Bring the right hand across the
abdomen to the right side of the waist. Both hands have the thumb on top
and the palm facing forward. Look straight ahead. (images 5.16a)

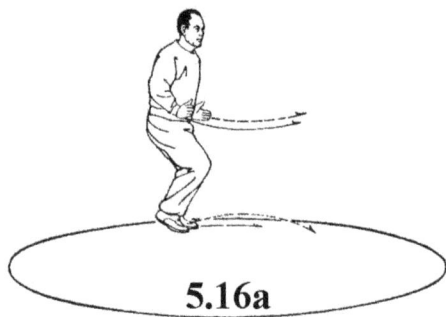

5.16a

5.16a

右足向前进一步，左足跟进半步，两腿屈膝，上身后坐；两掌同时
向前屈肘推出，掌腕相并，拇指外侧都向上；眼看两掌。

Step the right foot forward then bring the left foot up a half step, sitting
back. Push forward with both hands, with the elbows bent and the wrists
together (thumbs on top). Look at both hands. (images 5.16b)

5.16b

5.16b

5.17　怀中抱月　　　　　huái zhōng bào yuè

Embrace The Moon In The Bosom (right)

右足向身后退回一大步，上身随着右转，左足尖里扣，两腿屈膝；右掌同时臂内旋从身前下降，反臂向前平举，至平举部位时臂外旋使拇指外侧向上，屈肘作抱腰式；左掌则屈肘收于左腰侧，拇指向后，其余四指在前，掌心向下；眼看右掌。

Take a large step backwards with the right foot, turning the body to the right, hooking the left foot in, and flexing the knees. Medially rotate the right arm and lower the hand in front of the body, turning the hand over and lifting it out to the front. Once the right hand is raised horizontally, laterally rotate the arm (turn the thumb side up) and flex the elbow to form an embracing posture. Bring the left hand in to the right waist with the thumb in back and the fingers in front, palm facing down. Look at the right hand. (images 5.17)

5.17

5.17

5.18　叶底藏花　　　　　yè dǐ cáng huā

Hide A Flower Under A Leaf (right)

左足向右足前方迈进一步，足尖里扣；两腿微屈，上身右转朝向北方；右掌同时臂外旋使小指外侧向上，拇指外侧向下，屈肘环抱胸前；左掌随之向右腋下平穿；掌心向上，屈肘环抱。

Hook in the left foot in front of the right. Bend both legs. Turn the body right to face North. Medially rotate the right arm (little finger side on top and thumb on the bottom) and flex the elbow with the forearm across the chest. Stab the left hand flat in under the right armpit (palm facing up) with the elbow bent. The arms form an embracing posture. (images 5.18)

要点：与第一掌第三动叶底藏花同。

Pointers: Turn the head to the right to look at the right elbow.

5.18

5.18

5.19   鸿雁出群   hóng yàn chū qún

Swan Leaves The Flock (left)

两足原地不动。上身左转；左掌从右肘下面向身体左上方（圆圈西
南方）移转上举，与头平齐；右掌同时臂外旋，随左掌转动，置于
左肘里侧；两掌成仰掌，眼看左掌。

Turn the body to the left without moving the feet. Turn and lift the left palm
from under the right elbow to head height at the upper left side of the body
(towards the South-west of the circle). Laterally rotate the right arm and
follow the left palm with the right, placing it inside the left elbow. Both
palms are now supine palms. Look at the left hand. (images 5.19a)

5.19a

5.19a

上动不停，左掌臂内旋，向身体左方转动，成竖掌；右掌随着臂内
旋，屈肘向左肋侧下按，掌心向下；上身继续向左转动；头随着左
掌向左方扭转，眼看左掌。

Without stopping, medially rotate the left arm and bring the hand around to
the left of the body, forming an upright palm. Medially rotate the right arm,
bending the elbow so that the right palm presses down by the left ribs with
the palm facing down. Continue to turn the body to the left. Turn the head
to follow the left hand with the eyes. (images 5.19b)

5.19b

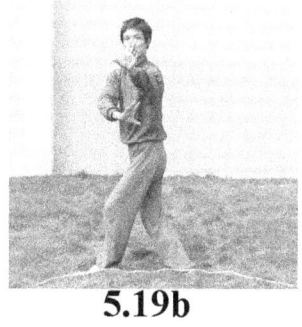

5.19b

第六掌

The Sixth Palm Change

左足尖外展，右足上步，开始从北向西，向南，向东，向北沿圆圈
行走一周。走到北方原地点如图时，再换接下一式。

Hook out the left foot and step the right foot forward. Walk around the circle in a westerly direction retaining the same upper body posture shown in images 5.19b. Follow the circle around to the North side then start the next movement.

要点：与第一掌第四动鸿雁出群同。

Pointers: Extend the left shoulder and elbow as far as possible to the left side of the body, with the left palm at eyebrow height. Push and press the right palm down and forward. Twist the waist to the left. Walk at an even pace.

6.1   紫燕抛翦   zě yàn pāo jiǎn

Violet Swallow Tosses Its Wings (right)

右足向左足前（西方）迈进一步，两足成倒八字步；左掌同时臂外
旋，使拇指外侧向上，从右臂上面向右侧推出，掌心向外；右掌伸
于左臂下面，小指外侧斜向上；两掌上下交迭；头向右转，眼看左
掌。

Hook in the right foot in front of the left (to the West), forming the Chinese character eight 八. Laterally rotate the left arm to turn the thumb side up, and push to the right above the right arm (palm facing out). Slide the right palm along under the left arm (little finger side on top). The arms cross, one above the other. Turn the head to the right, looking at the left hand. (images 6.1)

113

6.1

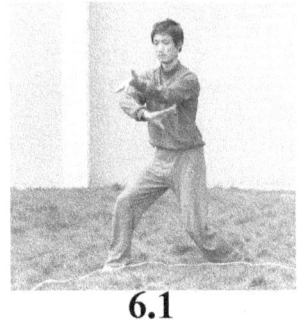

6.1

要点：与第一掌第五动紫燕抛翦同。

Pointers: Relax the shoulders, waist, and hips. Hold the arms in front of the chest in an embracing posture – do not cross them too tightly.

6.2   犀牛望月   xī niú wàng yuè

Rhinoceros Gazes At The Moon (left)

左足向左移动半步，上身稍向左转，左掌同时屈肘向左侧上方横架上举，拇指外侧向下，掌心向外；右掌同时臂外旋使掌心向左，掌指向下，屈肘向左推出；眼看左掌。

Shift the left foot a half step to the left and turn the torso slightly to the left. Flex the left elbow and block up from the left side with the left forearm horizontal (thumb edge on the bottom and palm facing out). Laterally rotate the right arm to turn the palm left (fingers pointing down) and push to the left with the elbow bent. Look at the left hand. (images 6.2)

6.2

6.2

要点：松肩松胯，左臂屈圆，右掌腕下屈。

Pointers: Relax the shoulders and hips. Form a circle with the left arm and flex the right wrist.

6.3   天王托塔   tiān wáng tuō tǎ

Heavenly King Lifts Up The Pagoda (right)

右足向左足前迈进一步，上身后坐，右掌向前屈肘上托，左掌同时臂外旋，屈肘使掌心向上，成托掌；眼看右掌。

Step the right foot in front of the left and sit back. Lift the right hand up to the front with the elbow bent. Laterally rotate the left arm (turn the palm up) and flex the elbow, lifting up. Look at the right hand. (images 6.3)

要点：左掌屈肘使小臂垂直，掌高与头平齐；右掌肘下垂，掌高与胸平齐。

Pointers: The left forearm is vertical with the palm at head height. The right elbow is dropped with the palm at chest height.

6.4   白蛇吐信   bái shé tù xìn

White Snake Spits Its Tongue (left)

右足尖里扣，上身左转，左足同时向左移半步，两腿屈膝略蹲；右掌随之向上，向里，向下绕一小圈，臂内旋使拇指外侧向下，掌心向右；左掌落于左肩旁，食指，中指并拢，余三指捏牢，掌心向上；眼看右掌。

Hook in the right foot and turn the body to the left, shifting the left foot a half step to the left and bending the knees. Turn the right hand in a small circle up, in, then down, medially rotating the arm (turn the thumb edge down with the palm facing right). Lower the left hand to the left shoulder with the index and middle fingers together and the others tucked in (palm up). Look at the right hand. (images 6.4a)

6.4a

6.4a

右腿伸直站立，左腿屈膝在身前提起，脚尖下垂；上身稍向左转；左掌指随之向身前屈肘指出，手心相上；右掌同时臂内旋，直腕使掌心反向上；眼看左掌指。

Straighten the right leg and lift the left knee in front of the body with the foot pulled in. Turn the body slightly left. Extend the left hand in front of the body with the palm facing up and the elbow bent. Medially rotate the right arm and straighten the wrist to turn the palm over to face up. Look at the left hand. (images 6.4b)

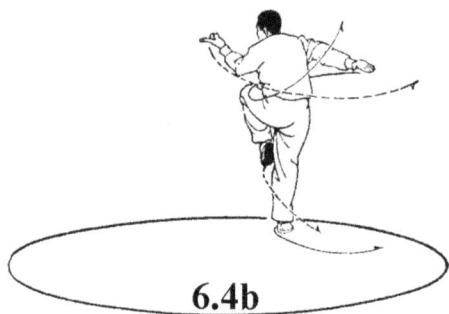

6.4b

6.4b

要点：右腿微屈，站立要稳；左臂屈成九十度角，左掌指高与眉齐。

Pointers: The right leg is slightly bent to keep balance. The left arm is bent ninety degrees with the hand at eyebrow height.

Translator's note: The first action is done turning the palm to press the back of the hand down, fingers pointing forward prepatory to the stab. The hand starts out near the throat, so it turns directly into the press down.

6.5   猛虎出柙   měng hǔ chū xiá

Fierce Tiger Escapes From The Cage (left)

左足从身后向东落步；上身随之从左向右转，面向东方，右足既向左足前迈进一步，两腿屈膝，上身后坐；两掌在转身使屈肘收于腹部，在右足上步时右掌向上屈肘穿出，成螺旋掌，小指外侧对向面部，左掌同时向身前推出，成竖掌；眼看左掌。

Land the left foot behind the body to the East, turning the body to the right to face East. Step the right foot in front of the left and flex the knees, sitting back. As the body turns, flex the elbows and bring in the hands to the abdomen. As the right foot steps forward, stab the right hand up in a spiral palm, the little finger side facing the head and the elbow bent. Push the left palm out in front of the body with an upright palm. Look at the left hand. (images 6.5)

6.5

6.5

要点：与第二掌第五动猛虎出柙同。

Pointers: Relax the shoulders. The right palm is slightly higher than the head. The right forearm is angled slightly forward. The left palm is at chest height. The left elbow is bent inside the right elbow. The palms are in line one above the other.

6.6   金鸡撒膀   jīn jī sā bǎng

Golden Pheasant Shakes Its Wings (left)

右掌从上由胸前屈肘下沉，叉于右腰侧，拇指在后，其余四指在前；左足同时向西北方伸出，左腿伸直；右足尖同时里扣，右腿屈膝下蹲；左掌随着左腿反臂伸出，掌心反向上；头随着左掌向左扭转，上身前俯，眼看左掌。

Bend the right elbow and sink the right palm down past the chest, placing it on the right waist (thumb behind and fingers in front). Step the left foot to the North-west and extend the leg. Turn the right foot in and squat on the

6.6

6.6

right leg. Roll the left arm over and extend the hand out along the left leg (palm rolled over to face up). Turn the head to follow the left palm and lean forward, looking at the left hand. (images 6.6)

要点：与第二掌第六动金鸡撒膀同。

Pointers: The weight is on the right leg in a left drop stance.

Translator's note: See my note with move 2.4.

6.7   移花接木   yí huā jiē mù

Move A Flower To Graft A Branch (left)

左足尖外展，上身直起，右腿伸直，右足随之进半步；左掌臂外旋使掌心向上，由下向上托起，成仰掌，肘微屈；眼看左掌。

Hook the left foot out and stand up, extending the right leg and stepping a half step up with the right foot. Laterally rotate the left arm (turn the palm up) lifting up in a supine palm with the elbow bent. Look at the left hand. (images 6.7)

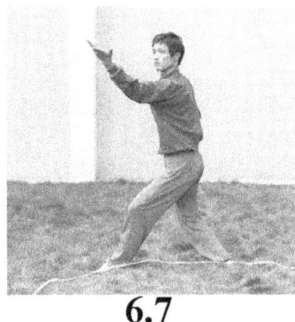

要点：与第二掌第七动移花接木同。

Pointers: Keep the head up, the strength balanced between the legs, and the left palm at head height.

6.8   脑后摘盔   nǎo hòu zhāi kuī

Pick A Helmet Behind The Head (right)

右足向左足前方上步，足尖里扣，成倒八字步；身体同时左转；右掌臂外旋使掌心向上，从右腰侧由左臂下面向左穿出；左掌位置不变，两臂上下交送；眼看右掌。

Hook in the right foot in front of the left, forming a Chinese character eight 八. Turn the body to the left. Laterally rotate the right arm (turn the palm up) and thread it out under the left arm to stab to the left. The left palm does not change position, so the arms are crossed, one above the other. Look at the right hand. (images 6.8a)

6.8a

6.8a

两足不动，右掌从左臂下面向右，向上斜摆上举，掌心仍向上；上体随着右转；左掌顺势屈肘置于右肘里侧；眼看右掌。

Without moving the feet, swing the right palm up from under the left arm to the right and up, with the palm still facing up. Turn the body to the right. Flex the left elbow to keep the palm inside the right elbow. Look at the right hand. (images 6.8b)

6.8b

6.8b

上动不停，右掌从右上方屈肘向脑后移转，至脑后时，向头顶上方托起；左掌从右肘里侧落至腹前，仍为仰掌；两眼平视。

Bend the right elbow to bring the palm down behind the head from the upper right. Once it gets behind the head, push up above the head. Lower the left palm to the abdomen, keeping it in a supine palm. Look straight ahead. (images 6.8c)

6.8c

6.8c

要点：与第二掌第八动脑后摘盔同。

Pointers: Lift the head, relax the shoulders and hips, and keep the elbows bent.

6.9 怀中抱月   huái zhōng bào yuè
Embrace The Moon In The Bosom (left)

右掌从身前落下置于右腰前，拇指向后，成俯掌；左足向左伸出，
上身随之左转；左掌同时屈肘向左掤出，拇指外侧向上，掌心向里，
作抱腰式；眼看左掌。

Lower the right palm in front of the body to the right waist in a prone palm with the thumb to the rear. Extend the left foot out to the left and turn the body to the left. Bend the left arm and press out to the left (thumb side of the palm on top and palm facing in) in an embracing posture. Look at the left hand.

要点：与第二掌第九动怀中抱月同。

Pointers: Bend the legs with the strength evenly distributed. Bend the left arm in a semi circle with the left palm at chest height. (images 6.9)

6.9

6.9

6.10 叶底藏花   yè dǐ cáng huā
Hide A Flower Under A Leaf (left)

右足向左前方迈进一步，足尖里扣；两腿微屈；上身左转朝向北方；
左掌同时臂内旋使拇指外侧向下；屈肘向左平带；右掌随之臂外旋
使掌心向上，向左腋下穿出。

Hook in the right foot in front of the left. Bend the legs. Turn the body to the left, towards the North. Medially rotate the left arm to turn the thumb side down, flex the left elbow and draw the palm across to the left. Laterally rotate the right arm (palm faces up) and stab under the left armpit. (images 6.10)

6.10

6.10

要点：与第一掌第三动叶底藏花同，唯方向相反。

Pointers: Turn the head to the left to look at the left elbow.

6.11   鸿雁出群   hóng yàn chū qún

Swan Leaves The Flock (right)

两足原地不动，上身右转；右掌从左肘下面向身体右上方（圆圈东南方）移转上举，与头平齐；左掌同时臂外旋，随右掌转动，置于右肘里侧；两掌成仰掌，眼看右掌。

Turn the body to the right without moving the feet. Rotate and lift the right palm up from the left elbow to head height at the upper right of the body (South-east of the circle). Laterally rotate the left palm and follow the movement of the right hand, keeping the hand inside the right elbow. Both palms are supine palms. Look at the right hand. (images 6.11a)

6.11a

6.11a

上动不停，右掌臂内旋，向身体右方转动，成竖掌；左掌随着臂内旋，屈肘向右肋侧下按，掌心朝下；上身继续向右转动；头随着右掌向右方扭转，眼看右掌。

Medially rotate the right arm and turn the hand to the right of the body to form an upright palm. Medially rotate the left arm and flex the elbow to press down by the right ribs (palm facing down). Continue to turn the body to the right. Turn the head to follow the movement of the right palm, watching the right hand. (images 6.11b)

6.11b

6.11b

右足尖外展，左足上步，开始从北向东，向南，向西，向北沿圆圈行走一周。走到北方原起点如图时，再换接下一式。

Hook out the right foot and step the left foot forward. Walk eastward around the circle holding the upper body posture as in figure 6.11b. Start the next movement after completing a full circle and returning to the North pole.

要点：与第一掌第四动鸿雁出群同，唯方向相反。

Pointers: Extend the right shoulder and elbow are far as possible to the right side of the body, with the right palm at eyebrow height. Push and press the left palm down and forward, twist the waist to the right, and walk at an even pace.

6.12 紫燕抛翦   zě yàn pāo jiǎn

Violet Swallow Tosses Its Wings (left)

左足向右足前（东方）迈进一步，两足成倒八字步；右掌同时臂外旋，使拇指外侧向上，从左臂上面向左侧推出，掌心向外；左掌伸于右臂下面，小指外侧斜向上；两掌上下交迭，头向左转，眼看右掌。

Hook in the left foot in front of the right (East), forming the Chinese character eight 八. Laterally rotate the right arm (thumb edge on top) and push out over the left arm to the left (palm facing out). Extend the left palm out under the right arm with the little finger side on top. The arms cross, one above the other. Turn the head to the left, looking at the right hand. (images 6.12)

6.12

6.12

6.13 犀牛望月   xī niú wàng yuè

Rhinoceros Gazes At The Moon (right)

右足向右移动半步，上身稍向右转，右掌同时屈肘向右侧上方横架上举，拇指外侧向下，掌心向外；左掌同时臂外旋使掌心向右，掌指向下，屈肘向右推出；眼看右掌。

Shift the right foot a half step to the right and turn the body slightly to the right. Flex the right elbow and block up to the right side with the forearm horizontal (thumb side on the bottom and palm facing out). Laterally rotate the left arm (turn the palm right and the fingers down) and push to the right with the elbow bent. Look at the right hand. (images 6.13)

6.13

6.13

Translator's note: In the photo, Cai Yuhua is already moving forward into the following move.

6.14 天王托塔   tiān wáng tuō tǎ

Heavenly King Lifts Up The Pagoda (left)

左足向右足前迈进一步，上身后坐，左掌向前屈肘上托，右掌同时臂外旋，屈肘使掌心向上，成托掌；眼看左掌。

Step the left foot in front of the right and sit back. Lift the left hand up to the front with the elbow bent. Laterally rotate the right arm to turn the palm up, and lift up with the elbow bent. Look at the left hand. (images 6.14)

6.14

6.14

6.15 白蛇吐信   bái shé tù xìn

White Snake Spits Its Tongue (right)

左足里扣，上身右转，右足同时向右移半步，两腿屈膝略蹲；左掌向上，向里，向下绕一小圈，臂内旋使拇指外侧向下，掌心向上，右掌落于右肩旁，食指，中指并拢，余三指捏牢，掌心向上；眼视左掌。

Turn the left foot in and turn the body to the right, shifting the right foot a half step to the right and bending the knees. Make a small circle with the left hand up, in, then down, medially rotating the arm to turn the thumb side down with the palm facing left. Lower the right hand to the right shoulder with the index and middle fingers extended together and the other fingers tucked in under the thumb (palm facing up). Look at the left hand. (images 6.15a)

6.15a

6.15a

左腿伸直站立，右腿屈膝在身前提起，脚尖下垂；上身稍向右转；
右掌指随之向身前屈肘指出，手心相上；左掌同时臂内旋，直腕使
掌心反向上；眼看右掌指。

Extend the left leg to stand up, lifting the right knee in front of the body
with the foot pulled in. Turn the body slightly right. Extend the right hand in
front of the body to stab with the two fingers (palm facing up). Medially
rotate the left arm and straighten the wrist, turning the palm over to face
up. Look at the right hand. (images 6.15b)

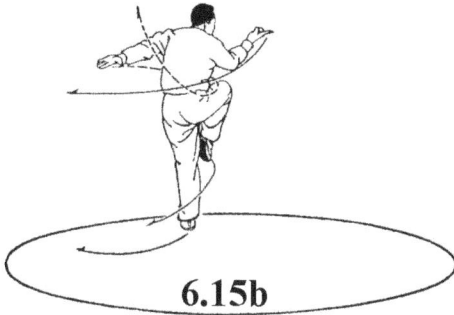

6.15b

6.15b

6.16   猛虎出柙   měng hǔ chū xiá

Fierce Tiger Escapes From The Cage (right)

右足从身后向西落步；上身随之从右向左转，面向西方，左足既向
右足前迈进一步，两腿屈膝，上身后坐；两掌在转身使屈肘收于腹
部，在左足上步时左掌向上屈肘穿出，成螺旋掌，小指外侧对向面
部，右掌同时向身前推出，成竖掌；眼看右掌。

Land the right foot to the West behind the body, turning the body to the
back to face West. Step the left foot in front of the right and flex the knees,
sitting back. As the body turns, flex the elbows and bring in the hands to the
abdomen. Then, as the left foot steps forward, thread the left hand up in a
spiral palm (little finger side towards the head). Push the right palm out in
front of the body with an upright palm. Look at the right hand. (images
6.16)

6.16

6.16

6.17 金鸡撒膀   jīn jī sā bǎng

Golden Pheasant Shakes Its Wings (right)

左掌从上由胸前屈肘下沉，叉于左腰侧，拇指在后，其余四指在前；
右足同时向东北方伸出，右腿伸直；左足尖同时里扣，左腿屈膝下
蹲；右掌随之顺着右腿反臂伸出，掌心反向上；头随着右掌向右扭
转，上身前俯，眼看右掌。

Bend the left elbow and sink the palm down past the chest, placing the hand
on the left side of the waist (thumb behind and fingers in front). Step the
right foot to the North-east and extend the leg. Turn the left foot in and
squat on the left leg. Extend the right palm out along the right leg with the
arm rolled over (roll the palm over to face up). Turn the head to look at the
right hand and lean forward. (images 6.17)

6.17

6.17

6.18 移花接木   yí huā jiē mù

Move A Flower To Graft A Branch (right)

右足尖外展，上身直起，左腿伸直，左足随之进半步；右掌臂外旋
使掌心向上，由下向上托起，成仰掌，肘微屈；眼看右掌。

Hook the right foot out and stand up, extending the left leg then bringing
the left foot a half step in. Laterally rotate the right arm (turn the palm up)
lifting up with a supine palm, the elbow slightly bent. Look at the right hand.
(images 6.18)

6.18

6.18

6.19 脑后摘盔　　　nǎo hòu zhāi kuī

Pick A Helmet Behind The Head (left)

左足向右足前方上步，足尖里扣，成倒八字步；身体同时右转；左掌臂外旋使掌心向上，从左腰侧由右臂下面向右穿出；右掌位置不变，两臂上下交迭；眼看左掌。

Hook in the left foot in front of the right, forming a Chinese character eight 八. Turn the body to the right. Laterally rotate the left arm to turn the palm up, and thread it out under the right arm to stab to the right. The right hand does not change position, so the arms cross, one above the other. Look at the left hand. (images 6.19a)

6.19a

6.19a

两足不动，左掌从右臂下面向左，向上斜摆上举，掌心仍向上；上体随着左转；右掌顺势屈肘置于左肘里侧；眼看左掌。

Without moving the feet, swing the left palm around under the right arm up to the left (palm still facing up). Turn the body to the left. Flex the right elbow to keep the right hand inside the left elbow. Look at the left hand. (images 6.19b)

6.19b

6.19b

上动不停，左掌从左上方屈肘向脑后移转，至脑后时，向头顶上方
托起；右掌从左肘里侧落至腹前，仍为仰掌；两眼平视。

Bend the left elbow to bring the palm down behind the head from the upper
left. Once it gets behind the head, push up above the head. Lower the right
palm in front of the abdomen, keeping it in a supine palm. Look straight
ahead. (images 6.19c)

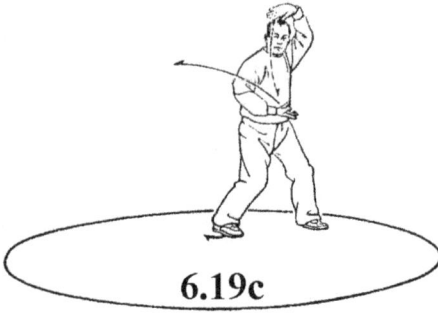

6.19c

6.19c

6.20   怀中抱月   huái zhōng bào yuè

Embrace The Moon In The Bosom (right)

左掌从身前落下置于左腰前，拇指向后，成俯掌；右足向右伸出，
上身随之右转；右掌同时屈肘向右棚出，拇指外侧向上，掌心向里，
作抱腰式；眼看右掌。

Lower the left palm in front of the body to the left waist in a prone palm
(thumb to the rear). Extend the right foot out to the right and turn the body
to the right. Flex the right elbow and press out to the right (thumb side on
top and palm facing in) in an embracing posture. Look at the right hand.
(images 6.20)

6.20

6.20

6.21 叶底藏花   yè dǐ cáng huā

Hide A Flower Under A Leaf (right)

左足向右足前方迈进一步，足尖里扣；两腿微曲；上身右转朝向北方；右掌同时臂内旋使小指外侧向上，拇指外侧向下，屈肘环抱胸前；左掌随之向右腋下平穿，掌心向上，屈肘环抱。

Hook in the left foot in front of the right. Flex the knees. Turn the torso right to face North. Medially rotate the right arm (put the little finger edge on top and the thumb edge below) and flex the elbow to place the forearm across the chest. Stab the left hand flat in under the right armpit with the elbow bent (palm facing up). (images 6.21)

6.21

6.21

6.22 狮子抱球   shī zi bào qiú

Lion Carries A Ball (left)

左足尖外展，上身随之左转向西，左掌从右腋下向前，向左屈肘平摆，掌心向上，成托掌；右掌同时从右胸前下沉，随即向头部上方屈肘托起，掌心向上，成托掌；眼看左掌。

Hook out the left foot and turn the body to the left to face West. Swing the left hand horizontally from under the right armpit forward then left, lifting up with the elbow and the palm facing up. Drop the right hand past the chest then lift above the head (palm facing up). Look at the left hand. (images 6.22)

6.22

6.22

第七掌

The Seventh Palm Change

左足尖外展，右足上步，开始从北向西，向南，向东，向北沿圆圈
行走一周。走到北方原起点如图时，再换接下一式。

Hook the left foot out and step the right foot forward, starting to walk
around the circle in a westerly direction. Complete a full circle in the same
upper body posture as figure 6.22. Go on to the next movement on
returning to the North side.

要点：右臂要屈成半圆，左掌稍过肩，两肩向下松沉函胸拔背。

Pointers: Form an arc with the right arm. The left hand is slightly higher
than the shoulder. Keep the shoulders relaxed and settled, settle the chest
and open the upper back.

7.1 狮子滚球 shī zi gǔn qiú

Lion Rolls A Ball (right)

左掌臂内旋，向身前屈肘平摆，右掌同时从上向身前下降，掌都
向西北方；眼看右掌。

Medially rotate the left arm and swing the hand horizontally to the front of
the body. Lower the right hand in front of the body (both palms face
North-west). Look at the right hand. (images 7.1a)

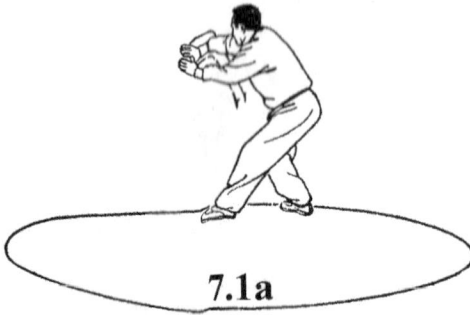

7.1a

7.1a

上动不停，两掌向右，向下，向腹前屈肘弧形摆动，至腹前时，两掌中指相对，掌心向下；眼向前平视。

Circle the hands right, down, then in towards the abdomen. When the hands come in to the abdomen, the middle fingers face each other and the palms face down. Look straight ahead. (images 7.1b)

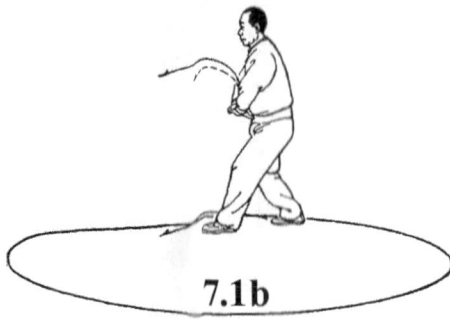

7.1b

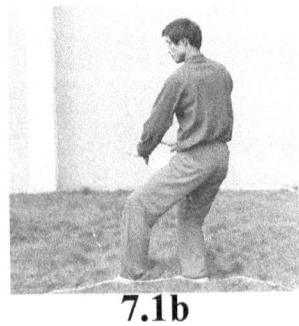

7.1b

要点：两掌按球状，头往上顶，两肩放松。

Pointers: The hands take the shape of pushing down on a ball. Lift the head up and relax the shoulders.

Translator's: Pull to the outside when the left foot is forward, then take two steps, left, bringing the hands in and finishing with the right foot forward for pounce.

7.2   狮子扑球   shī zi pū qiú

Lion Pounces On a Ball (right)

右足向左近进一步，两腿屈膝，上身后坐；两掌同时从腹部屈肘提于胸至胸部时，两掌向上，向前按掌扑出，掌心向下，成俯掌；右足上下相对，与胸平齐；左掌在右肘里侧，微低于右掌；内微屈；眼看右掌。

Step the right foot in front of the left, bending both knees and sitting back. Flex the elbows and lift the hands up in front of the chest, then turn the palms up and pounce out to push down to the front (palms facing down in prone palms). The right hand is opposite the right foot at chest height – the left hand is inside the right elbow, slightly lower than the right hand. Both elbows are slightly bent. Look at the right hand. (images 7.2)

7.2

7.2

要点：松肩沉肘，函胸拔背。

Pointers: Relax the shoulders and sink the elbows, settle the chest and spread the upper back.

7.3   狮子张嘴   shī zi zhāng zuǐ
       Lion Opens Its Mouth (right)

上身左转向东，左足随之前进半步，右足跟进半步，左腿膝微屈，右腿伸直；两掌在转身时，屈肘收于腹部；在转身后左掌臂外旋，屈肘上举，小指外侧向里，掌指向上；右掌同时向前屈肘平伸托出，掌心向上，掌指向前下方；眼看右掌。

Turn the body to the left to face East, stepping the left foot a half step forward and the right foot a half step in towards it. Flex the left knee slightly and straighten the right. As the body turns, flex the elbows and bring the hands in to the abdomen. After the body turns, laterally rotate the left arm, flex the elbow and raise the hand (little finger edge in the inside and the fingers pointing up). Flex the right elbow and extend the hand out to lift with the palm facing up and the fingers pointing to the lower front. Look at the right hand. (images 7.3)

7.3

7.3

要点：松肩沉肘，着力在右掌；左小臂上举垂直，左掌稍高过头；右臂微屈，右掌与胸平齐。

Pointers: Relax the shoulders and drop the elbows, putting power into the right hand. The left forearm is vertical, the hand higher than the head. The right arm is slightly bent, and the hand is at chest height.

7.4   狮子反身   shī zi fǎn shēn

Lion Rolls Over (right)

右足向左足前迈进一步，足尖里扣；上身随之左转对向东北；右掌同时向正东前方屈肘托起，掌心向上，掌指向前；左掌随之从上落于右肘下方，拇指外侧向下，掌心向前；眼看右掌。

Hook in the right foot in front of the left. Turn the body to the left to face North-east. Flex the right elbow and lift the hand to the front (East) with the palm facing up and the fingers pointing forward. Lower the left hand underneath the right elbow (thumb side down and the palm facing forward). Look at the right hand. (images 7.4a)

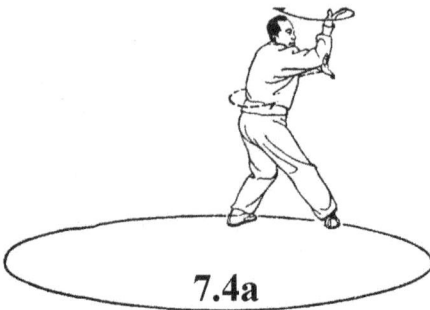

7.4a

7.4a

上动不停，上身左转对向西北；右掌屈肘在头部上方向后，向左平绕，停于左额上方，掌心仍向上；左掌随之向下，向身后绕行，至身后时，掌心向后，掌指向右；眼看左前方。

Turn the body left to face North-west. Bend the right arm and circle the hand above the head to the back then left, stopping by the left temple (palm still facing up). Circle the left hand down then to the rear of the body – once the palm is behind the body the palm faces back and the fingers point right. Look to the left. (images 7.4b)

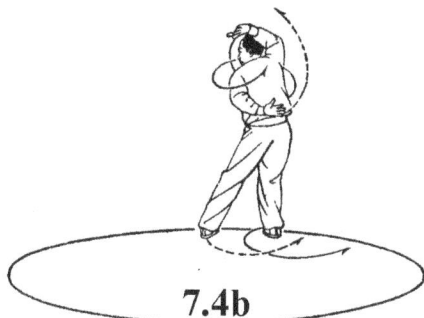

7.4b

7.4b

要点：在第一动时，右臂屈成九十度角，小臂要垂直，右掌微高过头；左臂屈成半圆，环护身前；上身重量大部坐落在左腿。在第二动时，两臂均屈，上身重量大部移坐于右腿。

Pointers: In the first part, the right arm is bent at ninety degrees with the forearm vertical and the right hand slightly higher than the head. The left arm forms a protective semi-circle in front of the body. The weight is mostly on the left leg. In the second part both arms are bent and the weight is mostly on the right leg.

7.5   狮子抱球   shī zi bào qiú

Lion Carries A Ball (right)

左足从身后偷步，身体同时从左向后，向东转，右步随之进前一步，两腿微屈，上身后座；右掌在转身的同时从上向下，向右腰侧，向后反臂伸出，随既臂外旋使掌心向上，从后向右屈肘平摆，成托掌；左则在转身后由身后从左向头部上方屈肘托起，成托掌；眼看右掌。

Step the left foot around back to the right, turning the body to the back to face East, then step the right foot forward. Flex the knees and sit back. As the body turns, bring the right hand down then to the right side, then back, rolling the arm over and extending it, then laterally rotate the arm (turn the palm up) and swing the arm horizontally from the rear to the right, lifting up with the elbow bent. When the body has turned, bring the left hand from behind the body from the left and lift above the head with the palm facing up. Look at the right hand. (images 7.5)

7.5

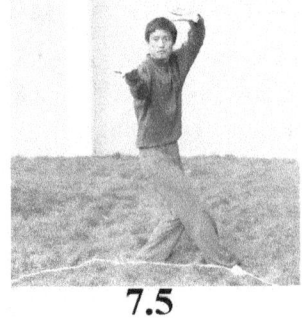

7.5

右足尖外展，左足上步，开始从北向东，向南，向西，向北沿圆圈
行走一周。走到北方原起点如图时，再换接下一式。

Turn the right foot out and step the left foot forward, starting to walk around the circle in a easterly direction holding the posture of figure 7.5. Go on to the next movement on returning to the North side after completing a full circle.

要点：与第七掌第二动狮子抱球同，唯方向相反。

Pointers: Form a curve with the left arm. The right hand is slightly higher than the shoulder. Keep the shoulders relaxed and settled, settle the chest and open the upper back.

7.6　狮子滚球　　　　shī zi gǔn qiú

Lion Rolls A Ball (left)

右掌臂内旋，向身前屈肘平摆，左掌同时从上向身前下降，掌心都
向东北方；眼看左掌。

Medially rotate the right arm and swing the hand horizontally in front of the body. Lower the left hand in front of the body (both palms face the North-east). Look at the left hand. (images 7.6a)

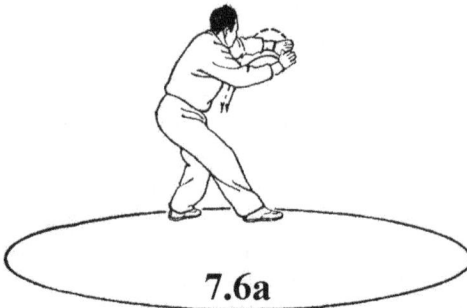

7.6a

7.6a

上动不停，两掌向左，向下，向腹前屈肘弧形摆动，至腹前时，两

掌中指相对，掌心向下；眼向前平视。

Circle the palms left, down, then in towards the abdomen. When the hands come in to the abdomen, the middle fingers face each other and the palms face down. Look straight ahead. (images 7.6b)

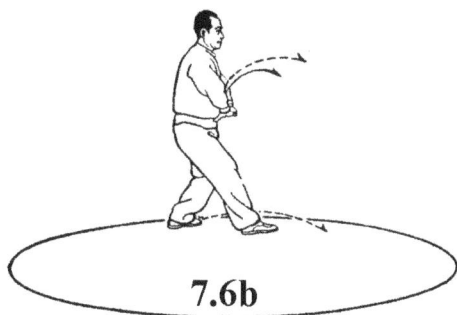

7.6b

7.6b

Translator's note: In photo 7.b, Cai Yuhua has already finished pulling in, and is turning the palms to raise them for the pounce.

7.7 狮子扑球 shī zi pū qiú

Lion Pounces On A Ball (left)

左足向右足前迈进一步，两腿屈膝，上身后坐；两掌同时从腹部屈肘提于胸部，至胸部时，两掌向上，向前按掌扑出，掌心向下，成俯掌；左掌与左足上下相对，与胸平齐；右掌在左肘里侧，微低于左掌；两臂部微屈；眼看左掌。

Step the left foot in front of the right, bending both knees and sitting back. Lift the hands up in front of the chest with the elbows bent. When the hands reach this position, turn the palms up then pounce out to the front (palms face down in prone palms). The left hand is at chest height above the left foot. The right hand is inside the left elbow, slightly lower than the left hand. The elbows are slightly bent. Look at the left hand. (images 7.7)

7.7

7.7

7.8　狮子张嘴　　　shī zi zhāng zuǐ
Lion Opens Its Mouth (left)

上身右转向西，右足随之前进半步，左足跟进半步，右腿膝微屈，左腿伸直；两掌在转身时，屈肘收于腹部；在转身后，右掌臂外旋，屈肘上举，小指外侧向里，掌指向上；左掌同时向前屈肘平伸托出，掌心向上，掌指向前下方；眼看左掌。

Turn the body to the right to face West, stepping the right foot a half step forward and the left foot a half step in. Flex the right knee and extend the left. As the body turns, flex the elbows and bring them in to the abdomen. After the body has turned, laterally rotate the right arm, flex the elbow and raise the hand (little finger edge in the inside and the fingers pointing up). Flex the left elbow and extend the hand to push out with the palm facing up and the fingers pointing to the lower front. Look at the left hand. (images 7.8)

7.8

7.8

7.9　狮子反身　　　shī zi fǎn shēn
Lion Rolls Over (left)

左足向右足前迈进一步，足尖里扣；上身随之右转对向西北；左掌同时向正西前方屈肘托起，掌心向上，掌指向前；右掌随之从上落于坐肘下方，拇指外侧向下，掌心向前；眼看左掌。

Hook in the left foot in front of the right. Turn the body to the right to face North-west. Flex the left elbow and lift the hand to the front (West) (palm facing up and the fingers pointing forward). Lower the right hand to below the left elbow with the thumb edge down and the palm facing forward. Look at the left hand. (images 7.9a)

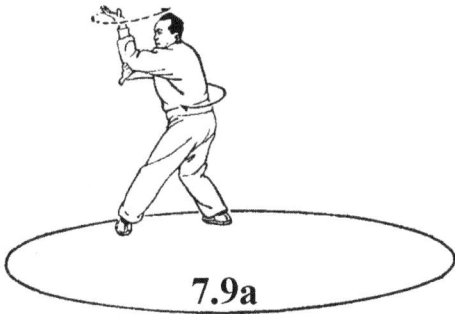

7.9a

7.9a

上动不停，上身右转对向东北；左掌屈肘在头部上方向后，向右平绕，停于右额上方，掌心仍向上；右掌随之向下，向身后绕行，至身后时，掌心向后，掌指向左；眼看右前方。

Turn the body right to face North-east. Bend the left arm and circle the hand horizontally above the head to the back then right, stopping by the right temple (palm still facing up). Circle the right hand down then to the rear of the body, so that the palm faces back and the fingers point left when behind the body. Look to the right. (images 7.9b)

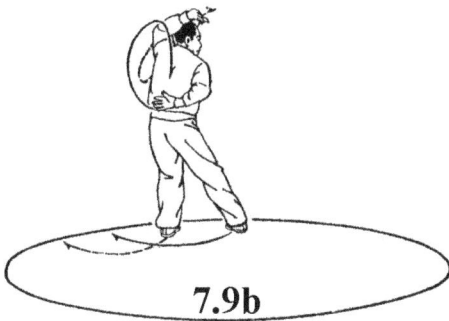

7.9b

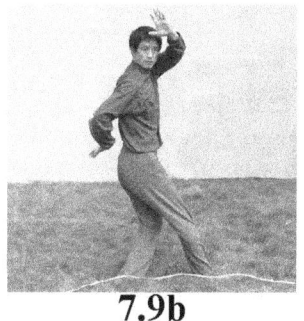

7.9b

7.10   天马行空   tiān mǎ xíng kōng

Heavenly Steed Soars Across The Sky (left)

右足从身后向左偷步，身体同时从右向后，向西转，左足随之前进一步，两腿微屈，上身后坐；左掌在转身的同时从上向下，向左腰侧，向后反臂伸出，随即臂外旋使掌心向上，从后向左，向上屈肘上举，小指外侧向里，掌心向上；右掌则在转身后由身后从右向上屈肘举起，随即由上从胸前屈肘下降，向左肘下方按掌，拇指外侧向里，掌心向下；眼看左掌。

Sneak the right foot around back to the left, turning the body around to the back to face West, then stepping the left foot forward. Sit back with both knees slightly bent. When turning, bring the left hand down, in to the left side, then roll the arm over and extend it to the back, then laterally rotate the arm (turn the palm up) and lift it from the rear to the left and up, bending the elbow (little finger edge on the inside and palm facing up). When the body has turned, bring the right hand from the rear to the right and lift it up with the elbow bent, then lower past the chest, pressing down below the left elbow (thumb edge on the inside and palm facing down). Look at the left hand. (images 7.10)

7.10

7.10

Translator's note: Complete the coil out of the preceeding move, stepping onto the circle line with the right hand lift up. The right hand may also cut across with the palm edge instead of lifting with the palm.

Then turn the body into the circle and move the arms to the walking posture. In the walking posture, the right forearm may be twisted to the extent that the palm faces into the circle, the fingers pointing down, so that it presses more out away from the body than down. Some do the left hand as a lift, palm up, and some twist it with the wrist straight, fingers up.

第八掌

The Eighth Palm Change

左足尖外展，右足上步开始从北向西，向南，向东，向北沿圆圈行
走一周。走到北方原起点如图时，再换接下一式。

Hook the left foot out and step the right foot forward, starting to walk
around the circle in a westerly direction holding the same posture as figure
7.10. Start the next move after returning to the North side.

要点：腰要向左拧转，两肩松沉。

Pointers: Twist the waist to the left and relax the shoulders.

8.1　马上开弓　　　　mǎ shàng kāi gōng

Pull A Bow Astride A Steed (left)

左足尖外展，右足跨进一步，两腿屈膝略蹲成马步；左掌同时从上
向右推出，掌指向上，掌心向右；两臂在胸前上下交迭，眼看左掌。

Hook out the left foot and stride out with the right foot, bending the knees
to form a horse stance. Push the left hand out from above to the right
(fingers point up and the palm faces right). The arms are crossed in front of
the chest, one above the other. Look at the left hand. (images 8.1a)

8.1a

8.1a

左足向左移动半步，右足跟进半步，仍为马步；右掌同时身体右方平伸削出，仍为俯掌，肘稍屈；左掌则经面部，向头部上方屈肘架起，掌心向前，拇指外侧向下；眼看右掌。

Shift the left foot a half step to the left and bring the right foot a half step up towards it, still in a horse stance. Extend the right arm to push to the right in a prone palm with the elbow slightly bent. Block up with the left arm, pulling the palm across the face then up above the head with the elbow bent (palm facing forward and thumb side on the bottom). Look at the right hand. (images 8.1b)

8.1b

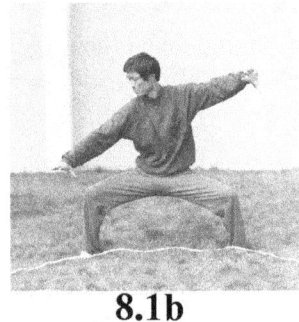

8.1b

要点：两掌的动作必须和两足的动作协调一致，右掌削伸与肋平齐，左掌上架稍高过头，身体中心坐落在两腿之间。

Pointers: The movements of the hands must be coordinated with those of the feet. The right hand pushes out at rib height and the left hand blocks up above the head. The weight is evenly distributed between the legs.

Translator's note: The first action may also be done stepping the foot forward, turned out, and sitting into a resting stance. The following move, then, is either skim jumped and landed in a horse stance or stepped back into a horse stance. In the horse stance, both arms may be fully extended, as Cai Yuhua has done in the photo.

8.2 金蛇般柳   jīn shé pǎn liǔ

Golden Snake Coils Around A Willow (left)

右足从身后向左偷步；两腿交叉屈膝略蹲；左掌同时由头部上方向右直臂伸出，掌心向右，掌指向下；右掌随之从右向左上方屈肘挑起，停于左耳旁，掌心向左，掌指向上；眼向东南方下视。

Sneak the right foot around back to the left. Cross the legs and squat. Extend the left arm down to the lower right (palm faces right and fingers point down). Lift up the right hand to the upper left, stopping beside the left ear (palm faces left and fingers point up). Look down towards the South-east. (images 8.2, and photo from behind)

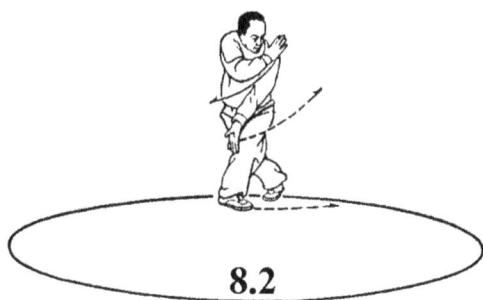

8.2

8.2

8.2 from behind

要点：两腿前后靠拢，右肘下垂，左掌贴靠左腿，两肩松沉。

Pointers: Tuck the legs in tight, drop the right elbow, keep the left hand tight against the left leg, sink the shoulders.

8.3 野马闯槽   yě mǎ chuǎng cáo

Wild Steed Charges A Manger (left)

左足向左移步，上身后坐，左掌同时向东南方直臂前撩，拇指外侧向上；右掌同时从左耳旁落下，置于右腰侧，拇指在后，其余四指在前，成俯掌；眼看左掌。

Shift the left foot to the left and sit back. Swing the straight left arm up to the South-east (thumb on top). Lower the right hand down to the right waist in a prone palm (thumb in back and fingers in front). Look at the left hand. (images 8.3)

8.3

8.3

要点：头往上顶，松肩松胯，左掌与左足上下相对。

Pointers: Hold the head up and relax the shoulders and hips. The left hand and foot are opposite one another.

Translator's note: The charge may be done as a slice (*liao*) or scoop (*tiao*). If slicing, the arm is straight and the thumb is tucked down, as in the drawing. If scooping, the arm is slightly bent and the wrist is cocked, as in the photo.

8.4   金蛇般柳   jīn shé pǎn liǔ

Golden Snake Coils Around A Willow (right)

左足尖外展，上身随之左转向东，两腿交叉，屈膝略蹲；右掌同时向左下方直臂伸出，掌心向左，掌指向下；左掌随之由前向右上方屈肘挑起，停于右耳旁，掌心向右，掌指向上；眼向东南方下视。

Turn the right foot out and turn the body to the left to face East. Cross the legs and squat. Extend the right arm down to the lower left (palm faces left and fingers point down). Lift up the left hand to the upper right, stopping beside the right ear (palm faces right and fingers point up). Look down towards the South-east. (drawing 8.4, no photo)

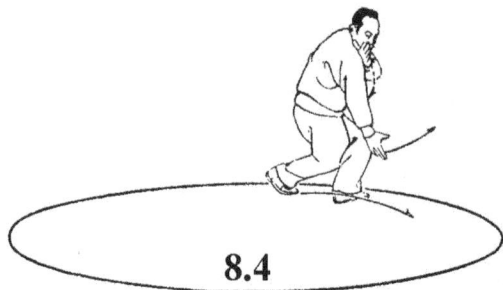

8.4

要点：与第八掌第三动金蛇般柳同，唯方向相反。

Pointers: Tuck the legs in tight, drop the left elbow, keep the right hand tight against the right leg, drop the shoulders.

8.5   野马闯槽   yě mǎ chuǎng cáo
Wild Steed Charges A Manger (right)

右足向东南方前进一步，上身后坐，右掌同时向东南方直臂前撩，拇指外侧向上；左掌同时从右耳旁落下，置于左腰侧，拇指在后，其余四指在前，成俯掌；眼看右掌。

Step the right foot forward to the South-east and sit back. Swing the right hand up with the arm straight to the South-east, with the thumb on top. Lower the left hand to the left waist in a prone palm (thumb in back and fingers in front). Look at the right hand. (images 8.5)

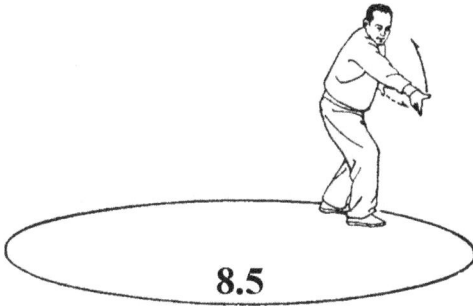

8.5

8.5

要点：与第八掌第四动野马闯槽同，唯方向相反。

Pointers: Hold the head up and relax the shoulders and hips. The right foot and hand are opposite one another.

Translator's note: This also is done either with a fairly straight arm as a slice up, or a fairly bent arm as a scoop.

8.6   刘海戏蟾   liú hǎi xì chán
Liu Hai Plays With A Toad (left)

两足原地不动，左掌向右臂下面伸出，仍为俯掌；右掌臂内旋使掌心向下，向身前，身左屈肘平摆；眼向前平视。

Without moving the feet, extend the left hand below the right arm in a prone palm. Medially rotate the right arm (turn the palm down) and swing it horizontally forward then to the left, with the elbow bent. Look straight ahead. (images 8.6a)

8.6a

8.6a

右腿屈膝在身前提起，足面绷平；左腿直立，膝微屈；右掌同时向
左，向上，向右，向下直臂绕行，停于右小腿前方，掌心向前，掌
指向下；左掌同时向下，向左，向上直臂绕行，至上方时屈肘横架
于头顶，掌心向上，掌指向右；眼向前平视。

Lift the right knee in front of the body with the foot pulled in. Stand up on
the left leg with the knee slightly bent. Circle the right hand left, up, right
then down with a straight arm, stopping in front of the left shin (palm faces
forward and fingers point down). Circle the left hand down, left and up with
a straight arm, then flex the elbow to block up past the head (palm faces up
and the fingers point right). Look straight ahead. (images 8.6b)

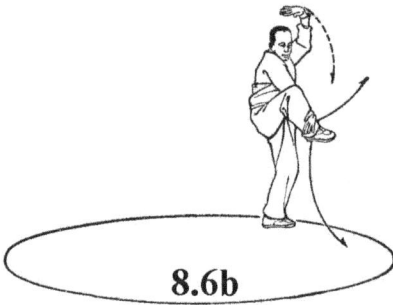

8.6b

8.6b

要点：两掌绕行必须协调，右腿尽量上提，左足站立要稳固。

Pointers: The hand circles must be coordinated together. Lift the right knee
as high as possible and stand steadily on the left leg.

Translator's note: Place the back of the hand on the top of the foot or ankle.
Do not pull the foot in tight, rather, pull the knee up with a feeling of
extending into the foot.

8.7   大蟒反身   dà mǎng fǎn shēn

Great Python Rolls Over (right)

右足向前落步，右腿屈膝，左腿蹬直，成右弓箭步；右掌同时向前
平伸托出，掌心向前，掌指向下；左掌由头部上方屈肘落于右肘上
面，掌心向前，掌指向右；身体微向前倾，眼看右掌。

Land the right foot to the front and flex the right knee, extending the left leg to form a right bow stance. Extend the right hand out to push out to the front with the palm facing forward and the fingers pointing down. Lower the left hand to above the right elbow with the palm facing forward and the fingers pointing right. Lean forward slightly and look at the right hand. (images 8.7)

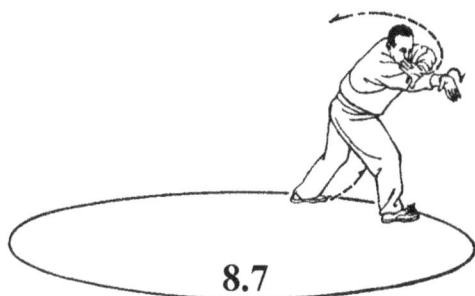

8.7

8.7

要点：两肩放松，全身中心在右腿。

Pointers: Relax the shoulders, put the weight on the right leg.

8.8   黑熊探掌   hēi xióng tàn zhǎng

Black Bear Stretches Out Its Paw (left)

右足尖里扣，上身左转对向西北，左腿屈膝提起，足尖下垂；右腿
伸直站立，膝微屈；右掌同时臂内旋，反臂举于身后，掌心反向上；
左掌随之屈肘上举，在头顶上方向后，向左，向前屈肘绕一小圈，
平举身前，掌心向上，掌指向前；眼看左掌。

Hook in the right foot and turn the body left to face North-west, lifting the left knee with the foot pulled in. Stand up on the right left with the knee slightly bent. Medially rotate the right arm and roll the arm over to lift up behind the body (palm rolled over to face up). Flex the left elbow and lift the hand up, circling above the head to the rear, left, then forward to end up lifted in front of the body (palm faces up and fingers point forward). Look at the left hand. (drawing 8.8b, photos 8.8a and 8.8b)

8.8a

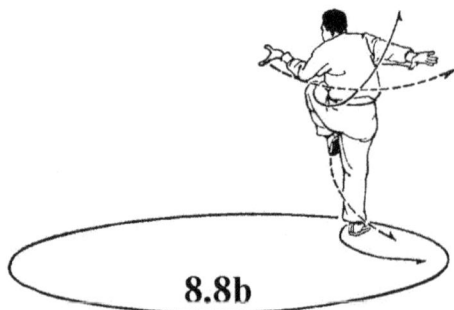

8.8b

8.8b

要点：站立要稳固，左掌高与眼平，两肩放松。

Pointers: Stand steadily. The left hand is at eye height and the shoulders are relaxed.

Translator's note: The rollover brings a curling chop to the left hand. Put power into the blade of the hand as you roll over, so the chop comes naturally.

8.9   猛虎出柙   měng hǔ chū xiá

Fierce Tiger Escapes From The Cage (left)

左足向身后落步，上身随之从左向后转，对向东南方，右足继之前进一步，两腿屈膝，上身后坐；两掌在转身时屈肘收于小腹前，掌心向上；在转身后，右掌向上屈肘上举成螺旋掌，小指外侧对向面部；左掌同时向身前推出，成竖掌；眼看左掌。

Land the right foot to the rear, turning the body back around leftward to face South-east. Continue on to step the right foot forward and flex the knees, sitting back. While turning, bring the hands in to the abdomen with the palms facing up. Then flex the right elbow and lift the hand, forming a spiral palm, the little finger side opposite the face. Push the left palm out in front of the body with an upright palm. Look at the left hand. (images 8.9)

8.9

8.9

要点：与第二掌第五动猛虎出柙同。

Pointers: Relax the shoulders. The right palm is slightly higher than the head. The right forearm is angled slightly forward. The left palm is at chest height. The left elbow is bent inside the right elbow. The palms are in line, one above the other.

8.10   金鸡撒膀   jīn jī sā bǎng
   Golden Pheasant Shakes Its Wings (left)

右掌从上由胸前屈肘下沉，叉于右腰侧，拇指在后，其余四指在前，左足同时向西北方伸出，左腿伸直；右足尖同时里扣，右腿屈膝下蹲；左掌随之顺着左腿反臂伸出，掌心反向上；头随着左掌向左扭转，上身前俯，眼看左掌。

Bend the right elbow and sink the right palm down past the chest, placing it on the right waist (thumb behind and fingers in front). Step the left foot to the North-west and extend the leg. Turn the right foot in and squat on the right leg. Roll the left arm over and extend the hand out along the left leg (palm rolled over to face up). Turn the head left to follow the movement of the left hand with the eyes, and lean forward. (images 8.10)

8.10

8.10

要点：与第二掌第六动金鸡撒膀同。

Pointers: The weight is on the right leg, forming a left drop stance.

Translator's note: see my note with move 2.4.

8.11   移花接木   yí huā jiē mù
   Move A Flower To Graft A Branch (left)

左足尖外展，上身直起，右腿伸直，右足随之进半步；左掌臂外旋使掌心向上，由下向上托起，成仰掌，肘微屈；眼看左掌。

Hook the left foot out and stand up, extending the right leg and stepping a half step in with the right foot. Laterally rotate the left arm (turn the palm up) coming up to lift up in a supine palm with the elbow bent. Look at the left hand. (images 8.11)

8.11

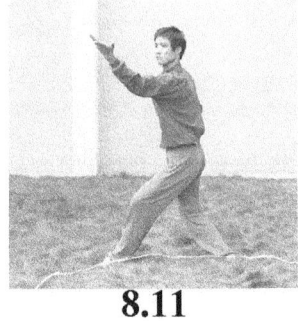

8.11

要点：与第二掌第七动移花接木同。

Pointers: Raise the head with the neck straight. Keep the strength evenly in both legs. The left palm is at head height.

8.12 脑后摘盔   nǎo hòu zhāi kuī

Pick A Helmet Behind The Head (right)

右足向左足前方上步，足尖里扣，成倒八字步；身体同时左转；右掌臂外旋使掌心向上，从右腰侧由左臂下面向左穿出；左掌位置不变，两臂上下交迭；眼看右掌。

Hook in the right foot in front of the left, forming a Chinese character eight. Turn the body to the left. Laterally rotate the right arm (turn the right palm up) and thread it out under the left arm to stab to the left. The left palm does not change position, so the arms are crossed, one above the other. Look at the right hand. (images 8.12a)

8.12a

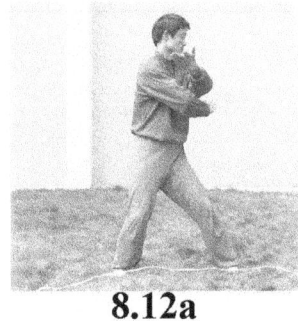

8.12a

两足不动，右掌从左臂下面向右，向上斜摆上举，掌心仍向上；上体随着右转；左掌顺势屈肘置于右肘里侧；眼看右掌。

Without moving the feet, swing the right palm under the left arm to the right and up, with the palm still facing up. Turn the body to the right. Flex the left elbow to keep the palm inside the right elbow. Look at the right hand. (images 8.12b)

8.12b

8.12b

上动不停，右掌从右上方屈肘向脑后移转，至脑后时，向头顶上方托起；左掌从右肘里侧落至腹前，仍为仰掌；两眼平视。

Bend the right elbow and bring the right palm down behind the head from the upper right, once it gets behind the head, push up above the head. Lower the left palm to the abdomen, keeping it in a supine palm. Look straight ahead. (images 8.12c)

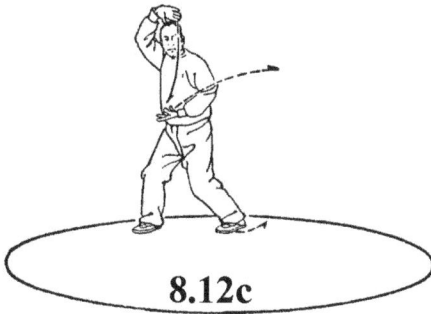

8.12c

8.12c

要点：与第二掌第二动脑后摘盔同。

Pointers: Lift the head, relax the shoulders and hips, keep the elbows bent.

8.13   怀中抱月   huái zhōng bào yuè

Embrace The Moon In The Bosom (left)

右掌从身前落下，置于右腰前，拇指向后，成俯掌；左足向左伸出，上身随之左转；左掌同时屈肘向左棚出，拇指外侧向上，掌心向里，作抱腰式；眼看左掌。

Lower the right palm in front of the body to the right side of the waist in a prone palm with the thumb to the rear. Extend the left foot out to the left, turning the body to the left. Bend the left arm and press out to the left (thumb side of the palm on top and palm facing in) in an embracing posture. Look at the left hand. (images 8.13)

8.13

8.13

要点：与第二掌第九动怀中抱月同。

Pointers: Bend the legs with the strength evenly distributed, bend the left arm in a semi circle with the left palm at chest height.

8.14   叶底藏花   yè dǐ cáng huā

Hide A Flower Under A Leaf (left)

右足向左前方迈进一步，足尖里扣；两腿微屈；上身左转朝向北方；左掌同时臂内旋使拇指外侧向下，屈肘向左平带；右掌随之臂外旋使掌心向上，向左腋下穿出。

Hook in the right foot in front of the left. Bend both legs. Turn the body left to face North. Medially rotate the left arm (turn the thumb side to the bottom) and flex the elbow to bring the hand across to the left. Laterally rotate the right arm and stab the right hand under the left armpit (palm facing up). (images 8.14)

8.14

8.14

要点：与第一掌第三动叶底藏花同，唯方向相反。

Pointers: Turn the head to the left to look at the left elbow.

8.15　天马行空　　　　　tiān mǎ xíng kōng

Heavenly Steed Soars Across The Sky (right)

右足前进半步，两腿屈膝，身体后坐；右掌从左肘下面向身体右上方移转上举，臂外旋使小指外侧对向面部；左掌同时向右移动，停于右肘下方，拇指外侧向里，掌心向下；眼看右掌。

Step the right foot a half step forward, sitting back with the knees bent. Turn and raise the right hand up by the left elbow to the upper right of the body, then laterally rotate the arm to turn the little finger edge opposite the face. Bring the left hand to the right below the right elbow (thumb side on the inside and palm facing down). Look at the right hand. (images 8.15)

8.15

8.15

右足尖外展，左足上步，开始从北向东，向南，向西，向北沿圆圈行走一周。走到北方原起点如图时，再换接下一式。

Turn the right foot out and step the left foot forward, starting to walk around the circle in an easterly direction. After returning to the North pole in the same position as figure 8.15, go on to the next move.

要点：与第八掌第一动天马行空同，唯方向相反。

Pointers: Twist the waist to the right and relax the shoulders.

8.16　马上开弓　　　　　mǎ shàng kāi gōng

Pull A Bow Astride A Steed (right)

右足尖外展，左足跨进一步，两腿屈膝半蹲成马步；右掌同时从上向左推出，掌指向上，掌心向右；两臂在胸前上下交迭，眼看右掌。

Turn the right foot out and stride out with the left foot, bending the knees to form a horse stance. Push the right hand out down to the left (fingers point up and palm faces right). The arms are crossed, one above the other. Look at the right hand. (images 8.16a)

8.16a

8.16a

右足向右移动半步，左足跟进半步，仍为马步；左掌同时身体左方
平伸削出，仍为俯掌，肘稍屈；右掌则经面部，向头部上方屈肘架
起，掌心向前，拇指外侧向下；眼看左掌。

Shift the right foot a half step to the right and bring the left foot a half step
in, still in a horse stance. Extend the left arm to push to the left with a prone
palm, the elbow slightly bent. Block up with the right arm, pulling the palm
across the face then up above the head with the elbow bent (palm facing
forward and the thumb edge on the bottom). Look at the left hand. (images
8.16b)

8.16b

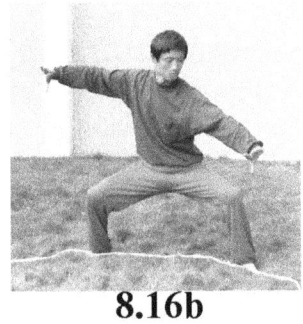

8.16b

8.17   金蛇般柳   jīn shé pǎn liǔ

Golden Snake Coils Around A Willow (right)

左足从身后向右偷步；两腿交叉屈膝略蹲；右掌同时由头部上方向
左直臂伸出，掌心向左，掌指向下；左掌随之从左向右上方屈肘挑
起，停于右耳旁，掌心向右，掌指向上；眼向西南方下视。

Sneak the left foot behind to the right. Cross the legs and squat. Extend the right arm down to the lower left (palm faces left and fingers point down). Lift up the left hand to the upper right, stopping beside the right ear (palm faces right and the fingers point up). Look down towards the South-west. (images 8.17)

8.17

8.17

8.18   野马闯槽   yě mǎ chuǎng cáo
        Wild Steed Charges A Manger (right)

右足向右移步，上身后坐，右掌同时向西南方直臂前撩，拇指外侧向上；左掌同时从右耳旁落下，置于左腰侧，拇指在后，其余四指在前，成俯掌；眼看右掌。

Shift the right foot to the right and sit back. Swing the right hand up to the South-west with the arm straight (thumb on top). Lower the left hand from by the ear to the left waist in a prone palm (thumb in back and fingers in front). Look at the right hand. (images 8.18)

8.18

8.18

8.19   金蛇般柳   jīn shé pǎn liǔ
        Golden Snake Coils Around A Willow (left)

右足尖外展，上身随之右转向东，两腿交叉，屈膝略蹲；左掌同时向右下方直臂伸出，掌心向右，掌指向下；右掌随之由前向左上方屈肘挑起，停于左耳旁，掌心向左，掌指向上；眼向西南方下视。

Hook out the right foot and turn the body to the right to face West. Cross the legs and squat. Extend the left arm down to the lower right with the palm facing right and the fingers pointing down. Lift up the right hand to the upper left, stopping beside the left ear (palm facing left and fingers pointing up). Look down towards the South-west. (drawing 8.19, no photo)

8.19

8.20   野马闯槽   yě mǎ chuǎng cáo
       Wild Steed Charges A Manger (left)

左足向西南方前进一步，上身后坐，左掌同时向西南方直臂前撩，拇指外侧向上；右掌同时从左耳旁落下，置于右腰侧，拇指在后，其余四指在前，成俯掌；眼看左掌。

Step the left foot forward to the South-west and sit back. Swing the straight left arm up to the South-west (thumb on top). Lower the right hand to the right waist in a prone palm (thumb in back and fingers in front). Look at the left hand. (images 8.20)

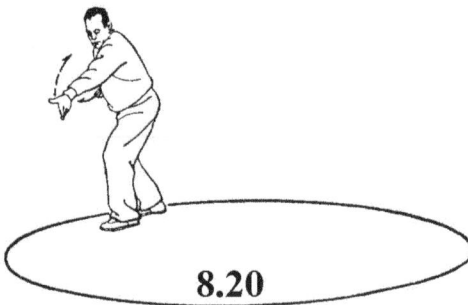

8.20

8.20

8.21   刘海戏蟾   liú hǎi xì chán
       Liu Hai Plays With A Toad (right)

两足原地不动，右掌向左臂下面伸出，仍为俯掌；左掌臂内旋使掌心向下，向身前，身右屈肘平摆；眼向前平视。

Without moving the feet, extend the right hand below the left arm in a prone palm. Medially rotate the left arm to turn the palm down, and swing it horizontally forward then to the right of the body. Look straight ahead. (images 8.21a)

8.21a

8.21a

左腿屈膝在身前提起，足面绷平；右腿直立，膝微屈；左掌同时向右，向上，向左，向下直臂绕行，停于左小腿前方，掌心向前，掌指向下；右掌同时向下，向右，向上直臂绕行，至上方时屈肘横架于头顶，掌心向上，掌指向左；眼向前平视。

Lift the left knee in front of the body with the foot pulled in. Stand up on the right leg with the knee slightly bent. Circle the left hand right, up, left, then down with a straight arm, stopping in front of the left shin (palm faces forward and fingers point down). Circle the straight right arm down, right, and up, then flex the elbow to block up past the head (palm faces up and fingers point left). Look straight ahead. (images 8.21b)

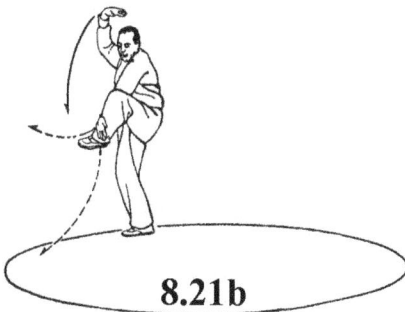

8.21b

8.21b

8.22   大蟒反身   dà mǎng fǎn shēn
　　　Great Python Rolls Over (left)

左足向前落步，左腿屈膝，右腿蹬直，成左弓箭步；左掌同时向前平伸托出，掌心向前，掌指向下；右掌由头部上方屈肘落于左肘上面，掌心向前，掌指向左；身体微向前倾，眼看左掌。

Land the left foot to the front and flex the left knee, extending the right leg to form a left bow stance. Extend the left hand flat out to push to the front with the palm facing forward and the fingers pointing down. Lower the right hand past the head to above the left elbow with the palm facing forward and the fingers facing left. Lean forward slightly and look at the left hand. (images 8.22)

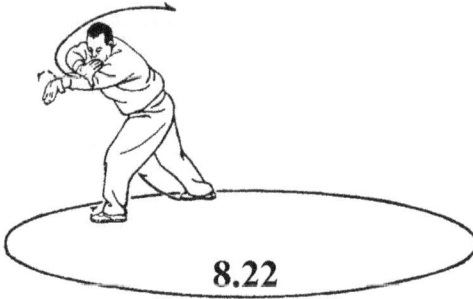

8.22

8.22

8.23 黑熊探掌   hēi xióng tàn zhǎng

Black Bear Stretches Out Its Paw (right)

左足尖里扣，上身右转对向东北，右腿屈膝提起，足尖下垂；左腿伸直站立，膝微屈；左掌同时臂内旋，反臂举于身后，掌心反向上；右掌随之屈肘上举，在头顶上方向后，向右，向前屈肘绕一小圈，平举身前，掌心向上，掌指向前；眼看右掌。

Hook in the left foot and turn the body right to face North-east, lifting the right knee with the foot pulled in. Stand up on the left leg with the knee slightly bent. Medially rotate the left arm and roll the arm over to lift up behind the body (palm rolled over to face up). Flex the right elbow and lift the hand up, circling above the head to the rear, right, then forward to end up lifted in front of the body with the palm facing up and the fingers pointing forward. Look at the right hand. (images 8.23)

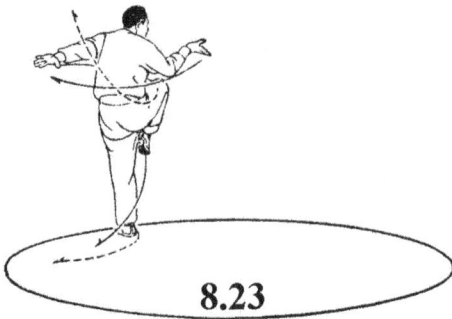

8.23

8.23

8.24　猛虎出柙　　　　　　měng hǔ chū xiá

Fierce Tiger Escapes From The Cage (right)

右足向身后落步，上体随之从右向后转，对向西南方，左足继之前进一步，两腿屈膝，上身后坐；两掌在转身时屈肘收于小腹前，掌心向上；在转身后，左掌向上屈肘上举成螺旋掌，小指外侧对向面部；右掌同时向身前推出，成竖掌；眼看右掌。

Land the right foot around behind the body, turning the body around to the rear to face South-west. Continue on to step the left foot forward and flex the knees, sitting back. While turning, bring the hands in to the abdomen with the palms facing up. After turning, flex the left elbow and lift the hand in a spiral palm with the little finger side towards the face. Push the right palm out in front of the body with an upright palm. Look at the right hand. (images 8.24)

8.24

8.24

8.25　金鸡撒膀　　　　　jīn jī sā bǎng

Golden Pheasant Shakes Its Wings (right)

左掌从上由胸前屈肘下沉，又于坐腰侧，拇指在后，其余四指在前；右足同时向东北方伸出，右腿伸直；坐足尖同时里扣，左腿屈膝下蹲；右掌随之顺着右腿反臂伸出，掌心反向上；头随着右掌向右扭转，上身前俯，眼看右掌。

Bend the left elbow and sink the palm down past the chest, placing it on the left waist with the thumb behind and the fingers in front. Step the right foot to the North-east and extend the leg. Turn the left foot in and squat on the left leg. Roll the arm over and extend the right palm out along the right leg with the palm rolled over to face up. Turn the head to follow the right palm and lean forward, looking at the right hand. (images 8.25)

8.25

8.25

8.26　移花接木　　　　yí huā jiē mù

Move A Flower To Graft A Branch (right)

右足尖外展，上身直起，左腿伸直，左足随之进半步；右掌臂外旋使掌心向上，由下向上托起，成仰掌，肘微屈；眼看右掌。

Hook the right foot out and stand up, extending the left leg to step the left foot a half step forward. Laterally rotate the right arm to turn the palm up, lifting up with a supine palm, the elbow bent. Look at the right hand. (images 8.26)

8.26

8.26

8.27　脑后摘盔　　　　nǎo hòu zhāi kuī

Pick A Helmet Behind The Head (left)

左足向右足前方上步，足尖里扣，成倒八字步；身体同时右转；左掌臂外旋使掌心向上，从左腰侧由右臂下面向右穿出；右掌位置不变，两臂上下交迭；眼看左掌。

Step the left foot in front of the right with the foot hooked in, forming a Chinese character eight. Turn the body to the right. Laterally rotate the left arm (turn the palm up) and thread it under the right arm out to the right. The right palm does not change position, so the arms are crossed, one above the other. Look at the left hand. (images 8.27a)

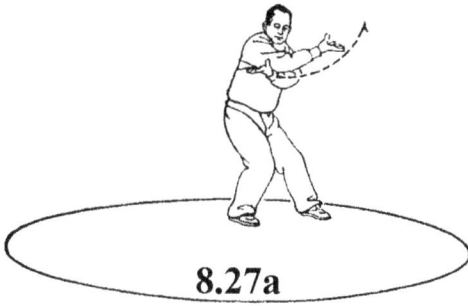

8.27a

8.27a

两足不动，左掌从右臂下面向左，向上斜摆上举，掌心仍向上；上体随着左转；右掌顺势屈肘置于左肘里侧；眼看左掌。

Without moving the feet, swing the left palm under the right arm to the left and up (palm still facing up). Turn the body to the left. Flex the right elbow to keep the palm inside the left elbow. Look at the left hand. (images 8.27b)

8.27b

8.27b

上动不停，左掌从左上方屈肘向脑后移转，至脑后时，向头顶上方托起；右掌从左肘里侧落至腹前，仍为仰掌；两眼平视。

Bend the left elbow and bring the palm down behind the head from the upper left. Once it gets behind the head, push up above the head. Lower the right palm past the left elbow to the abdomen, keeping it in a supine palm. Look straight ahead. (images 8.27c)

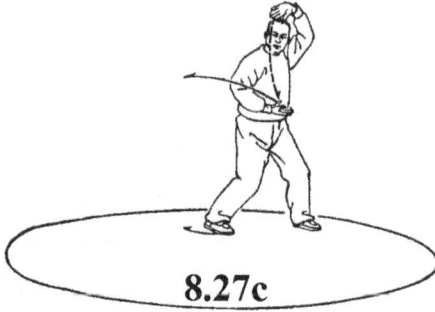

8.27c

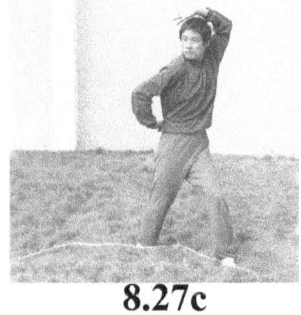

8.27c

8.28 怀中抱月   huái zhōng bào yuè

Embrace The Moon In The Bosom (right)

左掌从身前落下，置于左腰前，拇指向后，成俯掌；右足向右伸出，
上身随之右转；右掌同时屈肘向右棚出，拇指外侧向上，掌心向里
作抱腰式；眼看右掌。

Lower the left palm past the body to the left waist in a prone palm with the
thumb to the rear. Extend the right foot out to the right, turning the body to
the right. Bend the right arm and press out to the right (thumb side of the
palm on top and palm facing in) in an embracing posture. Look at the right
hand. (images 8.28)

8.28

8.28

8.29 叶底藏花   yè dǐ cáng huā

Hide A Flower Under A Leaf (right)

左足向右足前方迈进一步，足尖里扣；两腿微屈，上身右转朝向北
方；右掌同时稍向右带；左掌同时向右屈肘平穿；掌心向上，成仰
掌。

Hook in the left foot in front of the right. Keep the legs bent and turn the body to the right, towards the North. Draw the right hand slightly to the right. Flex the left elbow and stab the left palm flat to the right with the palm facing up in a supine palm. (images 8.29)

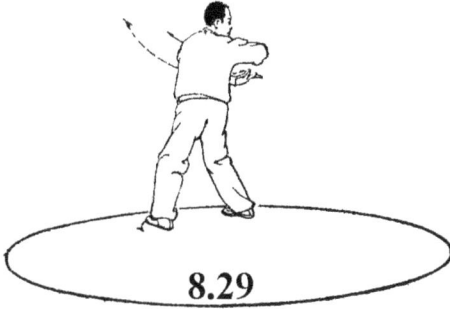

8.29

8.29

8.30   鸿雁出群   hóng yàn chū qún

Swan Leaves The Flock (left)

两足原地不动。上身左转；左掌从右肘下面向身体左上方（圆圈西南方）移转上举，与头平齐；右掌同时臂外旋，随左掌转动，置于左肘里侧；两掌成仰掌，眼看左掌。

Turn the body to the left without moving the feet. Rotate and lift the left palm from below the right elbow towards the upper left of the body (South-west) to head height. Laterally rotate the right arm and follow the movement of the left, keeping the hand inside the left elbow. Both palms form supine palms. Look at the left hand. (images 8.30a)

8.30a

8.30a

上动不停，左掌臂内旋，向身体左方转动，成竖掌；右掌随着臂内旋，屈肘向左肋侧下按，掌心向下；上身继续向左转动；头随着左掌向左方扭转，眼看左掌。

Medially rotate the left arm and turn the hand to the left of the body forming an upright palm. Medially rotate the right arm and flex the elbow to press the palm down by the left ribs with the palm facing down. Continue to turn the body to the left. Follow the movement of the left hand with the eyes, turning the head left. (images 8.30b)

8.30b

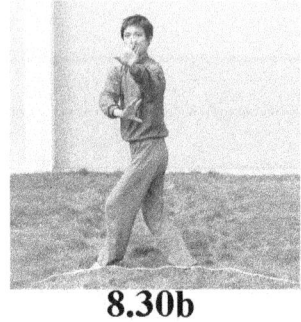

8.30b

8.31 收式   shōu shì

Close The Form

身体直起，面向西方，左足向右足并步靠拢，两掌下垂贴靠两腿侧，成立正姿势。

Stand up facing West. Bring the left foot in beside the right, lower the hands by the legs, standing at attention. (images 8.31)

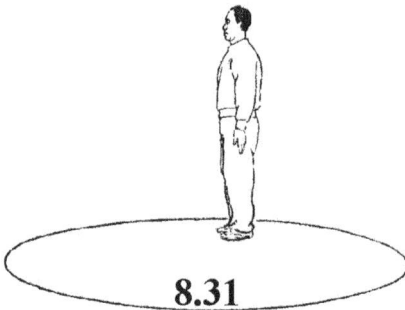

8.31

8.31

PRONUNCIATION OF PINYIN, THE CHINESE NATIONAL PHONETIC ALPHABET (WITH INTERNATIONAL PHONETIC ALPHABET EQUIVALENTS)

INITIALS (words can start with these consonants, or have a zero initial)		
PINYIN	IPA	ROUGH PRONUNCIATION GUIDE
p	p^h	Like English pet with a considerable puff of air.
b	p	Similar to the *pinyin* "p" but without the puff of air (unvoiced, neither English pet nor bet).
t	t^h	Like English tag with a considerable puff of air.
d	t	Similar to the *pinyin* "t" but with no puff of air (unvoiced, not dog).
k	k^h	Like English kill with a considerable puff of air.
g	k	Similar to the *pinyin* "k" but with no puff of air (unvoiced, not English get).
c	ts^h	Like exaggerating English cats.
z	ts	Like the *pinyin* "c" but without the puff of air (unvoiced).
ch	$tʂ^h$	Somewhat similar to English chat with a puff of air, but with the tip of the tongue rolled back.
zh	tʂ	Like the *pinyin* "ch" but with no puff of air (unvoiced).
q	$tþ^h$	Somewhat similar to English chat with a puff of air, but with the front of the tongue raised and the tip on the lower teeth.
j	tþ	Like the *pinyin* "q" but without the puff of air (unvoiced).
m	m	Like English met.
n	n	Like English net.
f	f	Similar to English fat, but with the teeth just touching lightly behind the lower lip.
s	s	Similar to English set.

165

sh	ʂ	Somewhat similar to English s<u>h</u>ow, but with the same tongue placement as the *pinyin* "ch" and "zh."
x	þ	Somewhat similar to English s<u>h</u>ine but with the same tongue placement as the *pinyin* "q" and "j."
h	χ	Raise the back of the tongue and let the breath come through the obstructed passage without vibrating the vocal cords.
l	l	Like English <u>l</u>et.
r	ɹ	Like the *pinyin* "sh" but with voicing.

FINALS

n	n	Like English pi<u>n</u>.
ng	ŋ	Like English si<u>ng</u>.

VOWELS

a	A a ɛ	Usually close to English f<u>a</u>ther (not p<u>a</u>t). Like y<u>e</u>t when written "-ian" or "yan."
e	ɣ e ɛ ə	Usually similar to English p<u>e</u>t, can tend towards a mid vowel.
i	i ǀ ɪ	Usually similar to English b<u>ee</u>. Similar to w<u>e</u>t when written "ui." After c, z, s, ch, zh, sh, and r it is similar to s<u>ir</u>.
o	o u	Usually close to English r<u>o</u>ll. Similar to c<u>ow</u> when written "ao," and <u>owe</u> when in "ou."
u	u y	Usually similar t English o b<u>oo</u>t. After the *pinyin* "x", "q", and "j" and in the vowel groups starting with these consonants, it is pronounced "ü".
ü	y	Similar to French <u>ü</u>. It is written after "n" or "l," because these are the only positions where both "u" and "ü" are possible
y	i	Partially like an English 'y', tending towards i.
w	u	Partially like an English 'w', tending towards u.

TONES IN PINYIN			
NUMBER	PINYIN	NAME	RANGE
1	ˉ	high level	55
2	´	high rising	35
3	ˇ	dipping	214
4	`	high falling	51
none	° or blank	neutral	in context

With tone sandhi, tones may change according to the preceding or following tone.

The tone marking is put over the main vowel when there are two vowels written together (usually involving the pronunciation of y or w).

About the Translator

Andrea Falk has practised external and internal Chinese martial arts since 1972. She has studied Chinese art, geography, history, language, linguistics, literature, politics, religion, and sociology since then, as well. She received a Bachelor of Arts majoring in Chinese (1977), a Bachelor of Physical Education (1979) and a Master of Physical Education with an emphasis on coaching science (1991) from the University of British Columbia. She trained in wushu full time on scholarship from 1980 to 1983 at the Beijing Culture Institute, earning an advanced studies diploma in wushu under the tutelage of professor Xia Bohua. There she learned the basics of Yang and Chen style Taijiquan, Baguazhang, Xingyiquan, Chaquan, Tongbeiquan, and modern Wushu (Changquan and weapons).

From 1984 she continued her studies in only the internal styles (counting Aikido as an internal style), and purely traditionally, visiting China on extended trips as often as possible. She trains Chen style Taijiquan, Jiang style Baguazhang, and Jiang Rongqiao's Taiji Changquan in Shanghai. In Beijing, she learns Xingyiquan and the Cheng, Liang, and Ma Gui styles of Baguazhang.

Andrea has taught the Chinese martial arts professionally since 1983. She founded the wushu centre in Montreal in 1984, in Victoria in 1992, and has been based again in Quebec since 2003. She travels to teach around Canada and Europe. For many years Andrea translated materials for her students, and in 2000 started tgl books to bring Chinese martial arts books to a wider audience.

tgl *books*

trois   gros   lapins   traversent   le   chemin

ISBN 978-1-989468-22-7

www.ingramcontent.com/pod-product-compliance
Lightning Source LLC
Chambersburg PA
CBHW030310100426
42812CB00002B/652